Latika Bourke was born in India and adopted by an Australian family at eight months. She is one of eight children all raised in Bathurst, NSW. In her hometown she began pursuing her dream of becoming a journalist, studying at Charles Sturt University and hosting a morning radio show on the locally owned and programmed station Radio 2BS. After joining Sydney radio station 2UE as a general assignment reporter, Latika was posted to the Canberra Press Gallery to report on federal politics in 2008. In 2010 she was named the Walkley Award's Young Journalist of the Year. Latika has previously worked for the ABC and now writes for the *Sydney Morning Herald* from Parliament House.

FROM INDIA WITH LOVE

GROWING UP AUSTRALIAN AND THE JOURNEY OF SELF-DISCOVERY THAT LED ME BACK TO MY INDIAN ROOTS

LATIKA BOURKE

ALLEN&UNWIN
SYDNEY · MELBOURNE · AUCKLAND · LONDON

This project has been assisted by the Australian
Government through the Australia Council for
the Arts, its arts funding and advisory body.

First published in 2015

Allen & Unwin
83 Alexander Street
Crows Nest NSW 2065
Australia
Phone: (61 2) 8425 0100
Email: info@allenandunwin.com
Web: www.allenandunwin.com

Cataloguing-in-Publication details are available
from the National Library of Australia
www.trove.nla.gov.au

ISBN 978 1 74237 773 5

Set in 13.8/19.5 pt Granjon LT Std by Bookhouse, Sydney
Printed and bound in Australia by Griffin Press

10 9 8 7 6 5 4 3 2 1

 The paper in this book is FSC® certified.
FSC® promotes environmentally responsible,
socially beneficial and economically viable
management of the world's forests.

To Mum and Dad—my real parents.

CONTENTS

Prologue   1

1   A wanted baby   3

2   Eight little Australians   23

3   A taste of the world   45

4   Newshound has *Slumdog* epiphany   67

5   A time of great and gradual change   95

6   My first taste of India   113

7   Coming 'home'   136

8   Pride, love and gratitude   165

9   Believing and belonging   191

Acknowledgements   213

PROLOGUE

The unexpected happened in Agra. A sensation I had never anticipated feeling about India stirred in my chest at the country's 'monument to love'—the Taj Mahal. Succumbing to the chaotic, intense, consuming, demanding magic of India at the Taj isn't just common, it's a cliché. But I'd spent years scornfully ignoring the country, determined to prevent this ever happening to me. India's crime? It was my first home. Yet now, after my first week in India as an adult, the first time I'd returned since leaving its soil at eight months of age, I was giving in to a mixture of feelings: pride, contentment, even a hint of joy and on top of it all a deep sense of reverence. In the old Mughal capital, the pride surged and I vowed to visit this country every year for the rest of my life. Maybe even live here. A transformation had taken place.

My history was never hidden from me, it was hidden *by* me. I'm as Australian as they come, 'Strayan' through and through, raised in small country towns—the kind where you didn't worry about locking the house, you waved to your neighbours when your cars passed, and childhood came with warnings to look out for drought-parched snakes in the swimming pool. Those were the everyday realities that I felt defined me, and I cherished them. Right into adulthood I rejected anything to do with the country of my birth. I wasn't just indifferent, I was hostile.

Even after I'd booked my flight, the thought of going to India didn't excite me, it terrified me. I scrambled through every possible reason for cancelling. After all, I'd only decided to go on the stupid trip because of a movie!

But there I was, gazing upon Agra Fort, and in that moment everything changed. I've stood before the Eiffel Tower, at London's great cathedrals, at Prague Castle and the White House and been awed by their grandeur—who wouldn't be? But in India I was more than just a tourist. What would be new sights and places to everyone else were my first, original homes. This building opened up the country as one of possibility where previously I had seen none. This was personal, meaningful, and for the first time I realised that I too could stake an ownership in this great country—something I would never have imagined when I was growing up in Bathurst.

1

A WANTED BABY

My girlfriends would giggle whenever I showed up to school events with my mum, Penny. There we were, the darkest girl in the class with the whitest mother in the room. Of course everyone knew why. It was no secret and there was no malevolence behind the laughter. It was clear to anyone who met us as a family that I was adopted.

There were eight of us kids all up. Five were Mum and Dad's biological children, and three of us were adopted—all three of us from India, and two of us from the same orphanage in north-eastern India, but we weren't related. If we Bourkes stood out as a family I never thought it was because of our differing skin colours. No, rather it was the large number of us and the logistical effort involved in moving us anywhere as a group.

And it was things like Damian's prowess as a cricketer and footballer, Rani's talent on the piano, Melissa's love of cooking, Mum's love of gardening, and Dad and Catherine's shared passion for horse-racing—continuing a long tradition on the Bourke side of the family. In other words, the usual preferences and inclinations that demarcate the individuals in any family.

In fact, my origins made so little difference to me that in my mind I always saw myself as white. If I look in the mirror I see, of course, dark brown eyes, black hair (that lightened as I grew older and not coincidentally after appointments at the hairdressers) and mocha-coloured skin (I once spent a whole day in the full sun with no sunscreen at a school swimming carnival to see if I'd burn like my friends, but only earned a flaky nose for my efforts). There were superficial differences, but I knew that inside I felt no different from anyone else.

So it was all the more galling when strangers said to me over the years, 'Where are you from?' Four words, with so many layers of meaning packed into them that left me mystified. Were they trying to say, *You look different to the rest of us. You obviously aren't one of us.* Who were they to ask, at any rate?

I hated that question so much, and so did Mum. Loathed it. Despised it. I deeply resented the presumptions that lay behind it. I detested the people asking it, whom I mentally labelled the Rude Inquisitors. Most of the time I knew they didn't mean any harm. They were perfectly well-intentioned, they'd just never thought through what they were actually signalling about me by what they were asking. But even if they were benign, that didn't make the fact that the colour of my skin was the initial and immediate prism through which they saw me any less infuriating. Sometimes I felt as though I could have been standing there wearing thongs, an Aussie flag-printed bikini, a blue cotton singlet and a trucker cap and still the first thing one of these people would say to me was 'So, where are you from?' And boy, were they persistent.

I'd usually start out with a curt 'Bathurst', hoping that might satisfy them. It rarely did. 'No, I mean where are your *parents* from,' they'd say. So I'd switch tactics. Force an exaggerated cheeriness I did not feel to send a warning that they had ventured beyond what was polite. 'Oh,' I'd say brightly, 'well, my mum's originally from England but she came here as a young girl, and Dad's Aussie but his grandparents were Irish.' I'd have a smile on my face but underneath I was boiling with anger as time and time again they totally failed to get the hint that I didn't want to satisfy their ignorant curiosity. 'No,' they'd say, spelling it out, since I was obviously a bit simple, 'what's *your* heritage?'

At this point I'd usually give up, resigned to the fact that whomever I was talking to had the social sensitivity of a brick wall and the indefatigability of a pit bull. I knew what they were asking. Why are you brown? But there were so many better ways to elicit the answer. Why not ask where my unusual sounding name 'Latika' was from? Or if I spoke any other languages. They could have even begun by asking if I'd been overseas before? These would have been far more elegant prompts for me to answer, free of the presumption that I looked different and therefore must not belong, or be a genuine Australian. If it wasn't done to ask people questions about their appearance at first meeting why was my skin colour always fair game? While I felt indignant I always gave in. It was easier.

'I'm adopted from India,' I would sigh, eyes rolling. Then, as though I felt compelled to provide a disclaimer to prove my Ocker-ness, I would hurriedly add, 'But I was adopted when I was a baby, so I'm completely Australian.'

Nature or nurture? That wasn't something I contemplated. I was a proud Aussie and I thought it showed in all that I was and everything I did. I didn't need to question it, so why did they?

In 1984, when I was born, my soon-to-be parents, Penny and John, were living in Berowra, nearly 10,000 kilometres away from north-eastern India. Technically a suburb of Sydney, Berowra is surrounded by national parks and waterways, giving it a semi-rural feel. John was himself one of nine children. His parents hailed from nearby Mount Colah, and how the family all fitted in the tiny house we visited each Easter and Christmas, with an ever-growing number of cousins, I'll never know.

Penny was from a much smaller family. It was just her and her brother, Andrew, and their parents. They had emigrated to Australia when Penny was seven, and her love of the English countryside soon transferred to the Australian bush.

John and Penny were both teachers, but they didn't meet in a classroom, they met through mutual friends on a blind date, and the rest, as they say, is history. They married and Melissa was soon on the way, followed by Catherine fifteen months later. And that was when they learned about a disease called cystic fibrosis.

CF, as it is commonly known, affects the exocrine system, which controls the respiratory and digestive systems, and among other things the disease brings a very high risk of lung failure. It's cruel and relentless, requiring treatments, medications, and physiotherapy several times a day. There is still no cure, and CF Australia describes it as 'the most common, genetically acquired, life-shortening chronic illness affecting young Australians today'.

Penny and John were told that their second daughter was likely to live for less than twenty years. (Life expectancy for people born with CF has more than doubled since then, to a median of forty-one years. My big sister is a living miracle: having received a double lung transplant in 2004, she celebrated her fortieth birthday in 2014.)

Catherine's diagnosis was a huge shock. There was no one else in Penny and John's extended families with the disease and they knew almost nothing about it. As they learned, it's passed on from parents, most of whom have no idea they carry the CF genes. About one in twenty-five people carry the genes, and both parents have to be carriers in order for a child to get the disease. When two carriers have a child there is a kind of CF Russian roulette: one chance in four that the genes won't be passed on at all and the child will be free of CF; two chances in four that the child will only get the gene from one parent, making them a carrier too; and one chance in four the child will have CF.

It was a devastating diagnosis, and also seemed to doom Penny's long-held dream of having a big family. But if my parents have one standout trait it's their tenacity. Penny began to explore other ways of having lots of children without the genetic risk of cystic fibrosis. She turned instead to the idea of adoption.

As Mum puts it, Catherine's diagnosis was the catalyst but not the only reason for our adoptions. I suspect that even without CF she would have considered the possibility. On the sea voyage to Australia when she was a child, her family had stopped over in Mumbai (then known as Bombay), and the memories of the children, many of them beggars and deliberately disfigured and in so much need, had stayed with her ever since. Dad was less enthusiastic about adoption but was won over by Mum's passion for the idea. So it became a question of how. India wasn't on the radar initially. Instead they looked to Vietnam.

In the previous two years, babies had come to Australia from South Vietnamese orphanages. As the war in Vietnam came to a climax in April 1975, this process sped up. In a mass evacuation dubbed 'Operation Babylift', around three thousand babies were taken out of the country, bound for Australia, the United States, Canada and France. But just over a fortnight after Babylift began, Saigon fell to the North Vietnamese and overseas adoptions were instantly stopped.

The next country Penny and John considered was Sri Lanka. But then they met a Catholic priest who had recently come to Sydney from Bangladesh. They told him of their situation and he said he could help. He put them in touch with a Bangladeshi orphanage and before long they began the process of adopting a little girl. Baby Mumtaz was all set to become the third Bourke child. The checks had been done, the paperwork on both sides had been completed and the authorities had given the all-clear. But just before Mumtaz was due to fly out, the Bangladeshi government changed its policy and forbade overseas adoptions. (Things have changed again since then. Currently, overseas guardianship is allowed, but only to people who hold Bangladeshi citizenship.) Talking about this years later, Penny was philosophical, telling me she firmly believed that Mumtaz 'was meant to be a part of someone else's family'. But at the time she was deflated.

Losing the chance to adopt after coming so close was very disappointing, but they didn't give up. A friend of Penny's knew of an Indian couple who were living in Australia but had managed to adopt from their home country. The friend suggested investigating the possibility of adopting an Indian child. Penny was initially sceptical, thinking that approval must have been contingent on the adoptive parents being Indian themselves. Still, it was worth looking into.

The friend was right: Indian babies were being adopted out to Australians. However, as they started down this new road, my future parents learned that their earlier enquiries about adopting from Vietnam and Bangladesh had made the Australian authorities suspicious of their motives. Were they 'baby shopping' (moving on from one country to the next because they were dissatisfied with the babies they were offered)? To anyone who knew Penny and John, this sugges- tion was beyond bizarre, but I guess I can see how it might have looked on paper. Of course, with a closer look at their situation, their sincerity and misfortune in trying to adopt to date were obvious. And so their first Indian adoption attempt got under way.

In 1980, and several long years after they had begun to look beyond Australia to expand their family, they held their new child for the very first time. (Back then all three of us were flown over, paid for of course by Mum and Dad but escorted by Indian guardians. Nowadays this would be unheard of!) She was eighteen months old and was called Pandeselvi. They renamed her but still opted for an Indian name, and one that was fairly popular: Rani, the Hindu word for queen. Penny was immediately captivated by the new baby. 'I spent the first six months just looking at her,' she told me.

But the adoptive parents had one more large hurdle to overcome. As was the usual practice then, the Indian authorities granted only temporary (twelve-month) guardianship. Reflecting the sexism of the times, it was granted to 'Mr John Bourke', with no mention of his wife, who couldn't relax for fear that someone would come and take her new baby away. During this trial period there were a number of home visits from both Indian and Australian officials to see how the child was fitting in and to check the quality of care she was getting.

Among the visitors were two nuns from the orphanage in Madras (or Chennai as it is now known) from which Rani had come. The adoption experience had been so smooth that Penny was soon keen to repeat it. The nuns, too, were delighted by how well it was working out and were happy to put her in touch with the nuns at St Mary's Orphanage in a village called

Fakirana in the city of Bettiah in a north-eastern Indian state called Bihar.

The process began again. This time both the Australian and the Indian authorities understood about the couple's CF risk and were satisfied about their motivation. Everything went to plan, and in August 1982 a baby arrived. It was the Bourkes' first boy; Penny loved boys' names beginning with D, and they renamed the baby Damian. Many years later she named their second boy Dominic, leading to much confusion: the wrong boy was constantly being summoned (which was useful if one of them was about to get into trouble for some mischief).

By late 1983, Penny was ready for another child. She wrote to the nuns at the Fakirana orphanage indicating that she would like to adopt another baby. After two successful and relatively easy adoptions, Penny thought she'd give the system one more try, although she was aware she was pushing her luck.

In theory, another adoption should have been simple. The family's bona fides had been well and truly checked, and all had gone well with Rani's and Damian's adoption. But Penny suspected that a third child might be too much of an ask for a family that had already been blessed with two babies; confirming this suspicion, the nuns warned her in a letter about a new government policy to prohibit adoptions to families that already had three or more children. However, the nuns knew that Penny and John were loving parents, and they were keen to give them a third child if they could do so without breaking the rules. They wrote back in December, saying that while they had no suitable babies at the moment, age-wise, they would try when one came in.

Three months later, a candidate appeared. It was me.

I had been delivered to the orphanage on 10 March 1984, the day after my birth. The nuns said that my grandmother and uncle had brought me in—they didn't say if they were kin of my birth mother or father, though I guess it was more likely they were from my mother's family. Scant information came with me, just that my mother was fourteen years old and my grandmother's eyesight was so bad that her son had to act as her guide. The only other thing I know for sure is that I was incredibly lucky to be brought in so quickly after my birth.

Bihar remains one of India's poorest states. At that point, nearly half its people lived below the country's official poverty line. It would have been so easy for a baby born into such poverty, in a family unable to care for her, to have starved to death. Instead, by a stroke of great good fortune, I was taken to a place where I would be fed and clothed and cared for until I could be placed with a family who would give me a hopeful future.

Almost from the moment of my arrival, the sisters earmarked me for the Bourkes. On my second day there, they photographed me and sent a copy off to Penny in Australia. Penny says that as soon as she saw the picture she was 'besotted'.

But two months later, nothing much had happened. In May, a Sister Gratia wrote from Fakirana saying, 'It is a bit difficult situation in India about the adoption matters.' As well as dealing directly with the nuns in Fakirana, Penny was communicating with Sister Hermann-Josef at the order's Delhi headquarters, the Holy Cross Orphanage. Following the required process, this was the facility through which Damian had earlier been transferred (at a cost of just a thousand rupees to Penny and John). A few weeks after Sister Gratia's letter, Sister Hermann-Josef wrote to clarify the situation:

> I put you on the list for adoptive parents, it is a so called 'waiting list' which I have to maintain since the Government has changed the rules for adoptions. Then you will have to send your documents here and this means when you have a child is on record for adoption I can propose you as the most likely parents. If Sr Gratia sends me a child for you I will naturally do this. But I also need to tell you ahead that there is a rule that we can only give children to families with less than three children.

This should have been the end of the road: Penny and John were over the number specified in the new rules. But Sister Hermann-Josef included a line that offered hope: 'There are though exceptions and we find occasionally a way.' She noted that the orphanage had to stick to the rules or they might lose their licence to facilitate adoptions. However, she added, she would try to ensure that Penny and John got their desired fifth child: 'I know children grow more harmoniously if there is a large family and there are children they are never doing well as single child.'

The waiting continued into June, and Sister Hermann-Josef warned Penny that more patience would be needed. She explained that special court approval would be required to break the rule for the maximum number of children. The local judge was said to be inflexible when it came to this law, and she had been told not to bother even applying to him, but she still had reason to hold out hope: she had convinced a judge to make an exception in a previous case.

Sister Hermann-Josef was evidently a patient, resourceful, determined woman. She went ahead and filed the application, advising the Bourkes that there would be a wait of around two and a half months before she knew the result. If luck was on their side and the adoption was approved, it would take about another month to organise a passport and visa. It was a long, demanding process, but, she added, 'All this is my work of helping one child to have a future and so I do it gladly.'

And yet despite this correspondence, it seems I might have become a Swiss baby. One letter, dated June 1984, between the sisters in Delhi and an agency in Vernier, Switzerland, that handled adoptions of Indian children, describes an attempt to find a suitable Swiss family for me. The European summer put paid to that idea, with the Swiss sisters writing back to Delhi: 'Unfortunately we have no family available right now for her, this being holiday season in Switzerland. And seeing her case is rather urgent, we do hope you will be able to approach some other agency in order to place her.'

The copy of this letter we have stands out from everything else in my file. In fact, it's strikingly odd, being the sole piece of correspondence in the bunch that didn't directly concern Penny and John. In hindsight, it could all have been done as part of the attempt to convince the Indian authorities that there really was nowhere else for me to go but Australia; a paper trail to satisfy the Indian judge that there were no other parents who would take me. Penny and John from Berowra were the best option, because the sisters made sure they were the only option.

In July, aged three months, I was transferred from Fakirana to Delhi, following the usual procedure for overseas adoptions, the nuns believing this to be the most likely outcome one way or another. Although photographs of me had been sent on ahead for my records, when I was delivered to the Holy Cross Orphanage there was consternation. Sister Hermann-Josef and the other nuns were immediately struck by the resemblance I bore to an older sibling pair already in their care—by coincidence, sisters who were in the process of being adopted by a Swiss family.

'It happens once in a while that we have children resemble one another. But this case is different,' Sister Hermann-Josef wrote to the Bourkes. She explained that the girls did have a baby sister but she had been lost before they reached the orphanage and so far searches had failed to find her. 'Now your child comes and we see the likeness, her behaviour, the way she cries, the way she feels when picked up is like the child [sic] we have for this Swiss family. On top of all this the elder girl says, "This baby is my sister."' Sister Hermann-Josef hoped Penny and John would understand that if it turned out to be true, the aim would be to keep all three children together, meaning I, too, would go to the Swiss family. But if that happened, she promised Penny and John, 'you would get from me a newborn child. Details and photos I will only send when sure which one. I know how we can get attached to a child when we have seen their photo.'

That was certainly true for Penny. She now had several photos showing my development as the months passed, and she already thought of me as her own. Sister Hermann-Josef herself had described me to the Bourkes as 'your baby'. Mum and Dad were praying every night for a breakthrough. Unlike with Mumtaz, Penny had seen my face, followed my development and let me into her heart. I was hers. She felt it. The nuns felt it too. It was just a matter of finding a solution.

Sister Hermann-Josef went to extraordinary lengths to find out whether I was related to the other two girls. She wrote to Penny and John that a sample had been submitted for 'a gene test'. Given that genetic testing as we now know it didn't exist then, and the nuns were unlikely to have had access to the versions that did exist, I wonder if she meant that a sample of my blood had been taken for comparison with that of the other girls'. She also wrote that she was travelling to the city of Lucknow where there were people who had known the siblings. Lucknow, the capital city of the northern state Uttar Pradesh, next to Bihar, was eight or more hours from Delhi by train—the return trip and tracking down the people she needed to talk to must have taken her at least two days. But she wrote, 'I can only be at peace if I did what is possible for me to place the child where I know is right.'

Penny and John were on tenterhooks until they received Sister Hermann-Josef's next letter in late July. It was the news they'd been praying for: I was not the missing sister. (I was moved to read in a later letter from the nuns that they had been able to find the third sister and reunite her with her two siblings. If you consider the Butterfly Effect—the idea that the tiniest actions can cause ripples of consequences—it's incredible to think how many lives these nuns touched.)

Penny and John also received an updated photo showing my development. In the accompanying note, Sister Hermann-Josef wrote, 'She is sixty-three centimetres and weighs five and a half kilograms she is not a dark brown child but light, fair as Indians like it. They would call her beautiful. She has soft dark brown hair.'

In all the correspondence from the sisters in Delhi and Fakirana, what stands out is their perseverance—their faith in themselves, their mission, their God and their purpose: to place the children in their care with loving families. But by August even the determined Sister Hermann-Josef was trying to prepare Penny and John for the fact that the chances of success were slimmer than ever. 'The news for you is not good, but not yet without hope,' she wrote. 'The registrar in the court told me to wait with your case, since he is pretty sure it will be turned down.' The stumbling block was the judge she had been warned about. 'This judge does not place children into families with more than two children and this is your fifth.'

There was another avenue, which involved waiting a few more weeks to try to have the case heard by a different judge. Beyond that, she advised, there was just one other, drastic tactic. 'Another way would be you wait will [*sic*] this present judge is transferred again in about ½ year's time. This would mean the child has to wait very long.' She asked if Penny thought it might be best to settle me with another family, even though 'since I gave you her photo I know you love her'. She also included an update on my progress. 'Latika is a very good child, always ready to smile if we come near her, and how she loves to be picked up and play with, she is also bubbling a lot and it seems she tries to tell her story.'

With the nuns running out of options, a slight quirk of my physical state came to the rescue. When I'd arrived at the Delhi orphanage I'd been a sickly child, notwithstanding the care I'd received in Fakirana. A report on my condition following my arrival in Delhi said I had trouble keeping down any food. By mid-August, a month later, my health had barely progressed and I was eating 'very little'. For some time I had been suffering 'fever, cold, cough' and, crucially, 'infected skin': I had some kind of spots or marks on my face and body. Whatever these were, they had been minor enough not to be noticeable in the photo and they hadn't stopped Sister Hermann-Josef calling me beautiful. But physical disfigurement was just the kind of thing that the judge would take into account.

A doctor wrote a letter for the court detailing my condition. He described me as having 'sores all over her body, inflamed and infected', and added, 'Due to these ulcers and boils she was smelling badly and was somewhat repulsive.' It was so bad, advised the letter, that I had to be kept in isolation from the other children. The upshot was, 'If this child could get a family who accepts her, gives her patient care, is not overanxious about her future looks and scars which might remain, she would have the best chance to heal.' He ended by writing rather dramatically, 'She would not be right choice for a single couple with no children. Instead if she could be among other children, this would be the best for the baby. I hope for the child's sake there might be [such a family] found.'

It still wasn't a foregone conclusion, though. Every day the nuns searched the court notices in the newspaper to see whether a date had been allocated for the hearing. They were anxious to get me into my new family. Despite my health, I was growing fast. 'So sad for me to say what progress they make when I know you should be watching them make it, and see their smiles and hearing their laughing, loudly now,' came one wistful letter.

By September I was showing the characteristics that anyone who knows me now would recognise. 'Latika tries to sit now, and she speaks and knows exactly what she wants,' wrote Sister Hermann-Josef. In lieu of the real thing, the sisters kept Penny and John updated with as many photos as they could supply. 'I tried very hard to catch Latika's beautiful smile but she gets serious whenever she sees the camera,' wrote a diligent Sister Hermann-Josef.

By October there was still no word, and Sister Hermann-Josef warned Penny and John that patience and faith were still needed; they weren't over the line yet: '. . . you will have to pray hard,' she wrote. 'They do not understand that a family can sincerely want so many children.'

In the end, the sisters' patience and determination paid off. The judge agreed that I was only fit for a kind-hearted large family where I could fade into the background. The official Child Study Report noted: 'Since the child had sores and an infected skin nobody else wanted her. No Indian family was ready to take her with this skin full of marks.'

On 7 November 1984, the first steps were taken to make it official. If all went well, I would be a Bourke within weeks. The High Court placed a legal notice on page two of *The Statesman* newspaper in Delhi to solemnly inform the general public that John Christopher Bourke 'and others' had filed as joint guardians of Miss Latika Bourke. I still have a copy of the newspaper. It smells like old books and is already sepia in colour. The notice goes on to declare that the High Court of Delhi advised all 'interested persons' that they had two days to show themselves to the court. Of course, nobody came, and my adoption was made official on 22 November.

Several days later, and eight long months after they had first cast eyes on a photo of me, I arrived at Sydney airport to be met by my new mum and dad and big sister Melissa. They loved the name Latika so much they didn't want to change a syllable. The name had been given to me by the nuns in Fakirana, who had written to Penny, 'Latika means a tender flowering climber—a loveable one.' Mum says that when I arrived she could just about make out the marks on my skin that had brought me to them. She instantly fell in love. And so did Melissa who had a bag of Smiths chips and begged Mum to feed them to me. Melissa recalls now she was fully expecting Mum to say no but she consented. I apparently hoed on in. Right from the start I was a happy baby, says Melissa.

2

EIGHT LITTLE AUSTRALIANS

Not long after I joined the family, we moved from Berowra to the bush. Home for the next seven years was a place too small to even really be called a town. It was a little cluster of properties known as Hobbys Yards, partway between Trunkey Creek and Blayney in the New South Wales central west. The official population during my time there was under two hundred. The Bourkes arrived as a set of seven but would leave as eight.

Our farm seemed enormous to me as a child. It was a place to stretch out, grow and breathe and feel that the entire world was yours to discover. The paddocks seemed to extend forever. If we little ones were venturing further than the shearing shed, it was always with a big kid or an adult, but there was plenty to see and do on your own. I happily made mud pies and climbed trees with my big brother Damian, and one year to our delight our favourite tree out the back surprised us with a tiny harvest of almonds.

The property boasted several dams (homes to leeches and yabbies) and room for horses, two brood mares. We kids rode them, but they were mostly Dad's personal passion—he's still a mad punter, although he's long since given away dabbling in the racehorses himself. We also had a goat, chooks, big vegie gardens, dogs Chuck and Tammy, and a solitary ram. Mum and Dad also kept a few sheep for wool and meat, and one highlight was the summer when some men were called in to help shear the sheep. Damian and I roamed around the shearing shed's numerous ramps, down which the poor old sheep had slid with comical inelegance, some with a ribbon of red streaming down their newly shorn skin. Dad had a big farm tractor—red, of course—and the property even had a cottage, complete with an open fire, separate to the main house, so friends from Sydney could come and stay.

For much of this time I was the baby of the family—Mum's nicknames for me were 'Teacup' and 'Tiki Burger'—and so had little to do with any of the day-to-day running of the farm. All I experienced were the fun parts: watching the shearers 'strip the sheep naked', scouting around the hayshed for stray eggs left by rogue chooks, and collecting snails for my glass aquarium. But looking back now, I don't know how my parents did it, given how much work it took to keep things ticking along.

When we first moved there, Dad was working in nearby Blayney, but he later began teaching at the all-girls Catholic high school Melissa attended in Bathurst, 80 kilometres away. Its full name was Diocesan Catholic Girls High, but it was colloquially known to one and all as 'Dio', and referred to by the more unkind as 'Dio Dogs', a moniker the school was desperate to be rid of (it would be renamed MacKillop College by the time Rani and I went there). The drive between Hobbys and Bathurst was about forty minutes each way, which meant long days for Dad getting to school and back, and for Mum looking after the kids and managing the farm. Mum and Dad weren't afraid of hard work, that was for sure.

For all the challenges, there were plenty of things Mum in particular loved about Hobbys, not least the winters, which were a lot more pleasant for her English genes than the hot, parched summers. Like Dad, she loved musical theatre, and our house was constantly filled with the sounds of Andrew Lloyd Webber's latest coming from Mum's record player. I knew the words to 'Memory' from *Cats* before I could even read.

My parents taught us early on to look out for each other, including on the school bus and in the playground. Family loyalty was non-negotiable. Dad was especially big on this. There was no greater crime we could commit, in his eyes, than failing to stand up for one another in public. Often this duty fell to Melissa, as the eldest. She never let the family down.

When I think back on that time in my life, the word that comes to mind is 'golden'. Not figuratively, literally. Golden was how it all looked to me: the hay, our paddocks, the land stretching away, the sun burning down on me, standing knee-high in the yellow grass. It seemed as though every other weekend Dad was out on his tractor, slasher attached, cutting back the grass. Mum brewed ginger beer in big square brown glass bottles the colour of burnt toffee. The flies live on in memory too. They were perpetual annoyances hovering around your face in the heat. At the start of the warm weather, strips of paper, glossy when brand new and as sticky as they appeared, would be hung near the back door of the house. They would soon be studded with trapped flies. But there would always be the few that made it inside, and then someone, usually Mum, would be on a mission with a fly swat making sure they didn't get into the kitchen.

The weather was a big part of life on the farm. Even on the coldest winter days in Sydney, the mercury tends to reach the teens. But we were on the other side of the Great Dividing Range from the coast, and snow was common in winter. Often we would wake up to find a massive drift had come in the night, making the land look like a huge cake someone had iced. We kids would bundle into coats and beanies and gumboots and trek off together squealing at the trick of nature that had made the places we knew unrecognisable. Mounds of gravel left by the side of the road by council workers would be transformed into snow dunes. We'd file back into the house red-cheeked and frosty to find Mum waiting, ladle in hand, with a giant pot filled with steaming porridge, which we topped with plenty of brown sugar, milk and cream.

At age five I lost my status as baby of the family when Mum fell pregnant with Dominic. By now it was 1989, treatments were improving, and Mum and Dad were ready to risk the possibility of another CF diagnosis for the opportunity to have another child. After the effort it had taken to get me, they knew there was no hope of another adoption. Dominic was born free of CF in September and his birth took us to six kids. Melissa, the eldest, was approaching the end of high school when he was born. She was focused on Roxette video clips on *Rage* and getting her first perm. She wasn't very interested in playing games with little kids, but I had Damian for that!

Mostly, if we wanted entertainment we made it ourselves. We hardly watched TV at all, but when we did it was one of the few things we all did together, given our age range. *Young Talent Time* was an early favourite of both mine and Melissa's. She would encourage me to perform my own routines, knowing it would drive everyone bonkers. Sure enough, before long I was banned from watching the show as a way of stopping the maddening impromptu concerts to which I would subject the rest of the family at every opportunity. Mum had put her foot down, but occasionally we'd sneakily watch an episode. Melissa now likes to raise these childhood embarrassments at large family gatherings whenever she wants a laugh, mainly at my expense.

Rani, Damian and I formed a sub-group, not because we'd all been adopted but because we were close in age. When Melissa and Catherine were growing up, the three of us were still primary schoolers, happy to spend hours racing billy carts, doing handstands and cartwheels and riding our bikes. Well, really Rani and Damian hung out together while I desperately tried to tag along. Rani was six years older than me, and Damian two. They could do cool older-kid things that I could only dream of, including barrel-walking—keeping their balance atop an old barrel turned on its side. I barely spent a second on the thing before I hit the ground, but they could keep going with what looked to me like the balance and coordination of circus performers. They were naturally coordinated and I was, let's say, better at reading, so their backyard accomplishments were the source of much envy to my young self.

Of course, like any older siblings they took full advantage of my desperate wish to be part of the posse. The pair of them had great fun with my endless gullibility, crafting elaborate tricks that I would fall for every time. One classic was their promise that I could have a prime spot on one of our favourite climbing trees for my very own if I just tugged on the rope dangling from a branch. A bucket filled with beautiful flowers would fall down, they assured me. I should have known, given that the tree was right next to a massive compost heap, that it wouldn't end well. Blinded by visions of being part of their club, I eagerly tugged the cord, and orange peel, apple cores and other decomposing delights thudded down onto my head.

Another memorable trick was made possible by the fact that we were a *very* Catholic family—we said grace every night at dinner and attended Mass every weekend. I knew exactly what taking communion looked like, but I had to wait until I took First Communion in year three to enter that grown-up club. Until then I had to wait in the pew and look on while the others went up to the front of the church, where the priest would administer what Catholics believe is the 'body and blood' of Jesus.

Lollies, like TV, were a rarity in our house this early on. Every so often our parents would come back from a shopping trip to Bathurst with a little treat for us. One day it was individual boxes of Smarties. Damian and Rani saw their chance. Ever eager to join in, I happily agreed when they proposed a new game, 'Communion'. Not only would they let me play, they would even give me the honour of being the priest. They, mere churchgoers, formed a continuous two-person loop in front of me as I dispensed Smarties. All mine, of course. I reckon it took about six of these occasions when I ended up with nothing but an empty box before I worked it out. Our early life was incredibly wholesome, so much so that even our mischief-making was more *Anne of Green Gables* than *Degrassi Junior High*.

It might sound odd coming from someone who now spends so much of her time online, but with every year that passes I'm more and more grateful to have had that upbringing. There was an innocence about it that simply isn't possible for children who have the internet and TV constantly at hand. Later on my parents bought a computer, but we kids weren't allowed to touch it. I didn't see a real video game until a friend got one, and when we eventually got Game Boys we had to share two between six kids and thought ourselves lucky to have them. If we wanted to re-listen to favourite songs we had to keep a blank cassette tape ready and hope they came on the radio.

But we didn't miss out. We used our imaginations. Dominic and I were especially close when he was little, and we'd take over the lounge room, building sheet tents that we'd sleep in for as many nights as Mum's patience would permit. I had a tea-party set and would invite one or other of my siblings for 'tea'. Mum would usually stump up some treats for my miniature plates.

We holidayed every year on the New South Wales south coast at Mollymook. These were some of the few occasions when I would succeed in roping the entire family into my favourite version of quality family time—games. I loved all board and card games. A particular achievement was beating everyone in Cluedo. Mum's proper English version of Monopoly, with its ancient crumpled pound notes, was put to good use as well, and we were all fans of Euchre. That was one of the few games Mum and Dad would play, giving me a treasured seat at the adults' table. Funnily enough, these are the things I still love to do now when I get the time and can rope someone into playing me. (Competitive, me? C'mon!)

At home, we spent most of our waking hours outdoors, running, climbing and exploring. We played backyard cricket and built huge bonfires then invited friends over to sit around them and roast marshmallows. These days it's not uncommon for me to spend an entire working week transiting from home to car to office and back via underground car parks without ever stepping outside. I wouldn't care to live on a farm again, I'm too much of a city girl now. But it was a great childhood: authentic and so Australian.

Melissa appointed herself my second mother. It's something I've noticed in other big families where the eldest is a girl and there's a big age spread. I adored being the one she doted on. Come shearing time on the farm, when Mum and Dad were safely occupied for long stretches down at the shed, she would whip up pans of thick gooey caramel. One of us was always posted as a lookout, and it was a furious, frantic exercise trying to hide all the baking trays full of cooling caramel on those occasions when the lookout spotted Mum heading back up earlier than expected.

My first two years of school were spent, with Rani and Damian, at a tiny one-classroom public school in the nearby village of Newbridge. The job of teacher came with accommodation on the grounds. The very kind and patient Mr Fisher taught about twenty of us, including his son and a number of other sibling groups like ours, ranging in age from kindy to year six. That funny little school was a fantastic introduction to education. There was rarely trouble. In fact, I can't remember any major arguments between us students, and on the best days the entire student body, from pre-teens to tiny newbies, would play together at lunchtime.

We would make up games over the underground water tanks and dare each other to go down to the back of the yard, where the most fearsome swooping magpies nested. We armoured ourselves by wearing the rubbish-bin lids on our heads—the old-style ribbed metal ones, which must have been well cleaned because fortunately they didn't smell. They made for surprisingly effective magpie deterrents! Fridays were the best. Everyone came to school with lunch money. We didn't need a school canteen; instead we all ordered meat pies from the local pub up the road, owned by the family of one of our classmates. I loved my time at Newbridge school.

But their workload was taking its toll on Mum and Dad, and eventually it became too much. When I was seven, our parents sat us down and told us they were selling the farm. Dad had just taken up a new job as deputy principal of a Catholic primary school in Bathurst. We were going to move closer to town, and Rani, Damian and I would switch to his new school.

Bathurst wasn't exactly a metropolis, but even so Mum preferred country life. So our new place was on an acre or so of land in Forest Grove, a hamlet of about thirty houses just past the Bathurst Sheep and Cattle Drome, fifteen minutes' drive into the town itself. Later on, as a teenager, I would detest living *so far out* (complete with dramatic eye roll), but when we first moved there, and for a good four or five years afterwards, I loved the continuation of the freedom we'd had on the farm.

At this stage Damian hadn't quite progressed to being too cool for his little sister, so he spent a lot of time as my buddy. Dominic was growing up too and becoming a fun little playmate. The new house came with a pool. I'd had some swimming lessons through Newbridge school but I still couldn't swim properly. Even though he rarely swam himself, Damian sat by the pool for a whole summer and verbally taught me how to swim, and several years later he and Rani finally taught me how to dive (instead of belly flop!).

The backyard, which looked out at the Great Dividing Range, was enormous. Damian enjoyed practising his bowling and kicking a footy, but my favoured pursuits were becoming more bookish. Mum, who had taught me to read, collected first-edition Enid Blytons. I read them. And reread them. And re-re-reread them. I still do. I lived in my imagination.

Back then, the worst thing that could happen was to be caught reading under my doona by the light of a torch after bedtime. Mum or Dad would confiscate the book, and it was excruciating punishment: I'd be dying to know how the Famous Five's latest adventure had transpired and would be forced to wait for up to a week before I found out. I'm pretty sure Mum and Dad were right—I ruined my eyesight reading in dim light like that. But when I was ten, finding out the end of an mystery adventure novel was an urgent priority compared to the glasses, contacts and eventual laser surgery I would fork out thousands of dollars for in my twenties. Dad kept the lawns mown beautifully, and I spent many days curled up in a grassy spot under the cherry tree out front, lost inside other worlds.

We still kept chooks, and Mum and Dad built a couple of aviaries for Catherine, who loved parrots, birds, rabbits and guinea pigs. In fact, she and Mum shared a love for all sorts of animals. One dog, Chuck, had died at Hobbys, but our beloved Tammy made the journey with us to Forest Grove. Spot, Daisy and Shadow all joined the canine contingent over time. Such big gardens also required a lot of looking after, of course, which meant there were plenty of chores to do, and some of these became my duties as I grew older—I hope I never have to weed again in my life!

As soon as we could walk, Dad taught each of us to scan the ground with every step. At the farm, we had been looking for tiger snakes, which are as venomous as they are aggressive.

In our new house the danger was eastern brown snakes. Tiger snakes are scary enough, ranking in the ten most venomous snakes in the world, but eastern browns leave them in the dust: they're second only to the taipan in the strength of their venom. And, boy, can they be aggressive.

Brown snakes were a perennial hazard at Forest Grove. Many a king brown fell victim to the next-door neighbour's 'snake gun' (a specially designed gun that uses shell ammunition and allows single close range shots) and to Dad's spade—even, on one memorable occasion, to the blades of his ride-on mower. Every year there would be at least one close encounter for someone in the family. Three times it was me. The first incident was scary but over quickly. We had just moved to Forest Grove so I was only seven or eight years old. I was playing along the pool fence in the backyard that looked on to paddocks and paddocks, against the backdrop of the mountains. Slithering along my feet was a snake. I looked down and started screaming. Mum and Dad knew exactly what was going on the moment I started screaming but yelled out that the snake would move on and that it would be okay. They were right. In the end no harm was done, and it was such a brief encounter that I soon stopped thinking about it.

But the second incident, when I was twelve, was unforgettable. By now we were a family of seven children: two years after we'd moved, Mum had given birth to another daughter, Gabriela. (The final member of the family, Joseph, would be making his appearance soon.) I was playing in the pool while keeping a big-sisterly eye on Dominic, then seven, and Gabriela, three, and two of their friends from up the road. I had been designated supervisor, an important job. We often looked after the younger kids while Dad was still at work and Mum was helping make ends meet by tutoring after school, and we took our responsibilities seriously. If anything happened on your watch there would be big trouble.

On this particular day, Mum and Dad were at home and just inside but being the oldest of the kids swimming it was my responsibility to make sure there were no silly antics. I was keeping the younger kids entertained by throwing in coins for them to try to find the fastest. So that I could join in the fun, I closed my eyes and chucked the coins as far as I could, then dived in too. When I opened my eyes underwater in search of a metal gleam, I spotted a dark hose in the water. There had been a few barneys of late about us kids leaving goggles and other assorted items in the pool, only for them to be sucked into the pool filter. 'Oh, those silly kids chucking a hose in the pool,' I thought. 'Dad will be so mad if it goes into the filter.'

Kicking my legs strongly, I dived down to grab it, at which point I realised it wasn't floating in a straight line but was undulating through the water. A slitted eye met mine. It was no hose. My reaction still surprises me. I can remember it clearly even today. I didn't scream, panic or flail. Instead, in one of the strangest moments of my life, I seemed to be looking down at myself from an angle as, swiftly but calmly, I swam to the other side of the pool, then firmly ordered the little ones out of the water. 'Everyone out, there's a snake in the pool.'

'Where?' one of them asked. Then, spotting it just a metre or so away, they all got out and ran towards the house.

I took off after them, but I was still more calm than I could have believed possible when I said, 'Mum, Dad, there's a snake in the pool.' I've never seen my parents move so quickly, before or since. At first, Dad tried to drown it, using the skimmer net to hold it under the water. Soon the net was sporting great rips where the increasingly angry creature had lunged with its fangs.

Mum must have called our neighbour, because he showed up and somehow he and Dad managed to get the snake into a big sturdy bag of the kind used to transport manure. It was swung into the outdoor freezer, and there it stayed, cooling off, until a trained volunteer from the wildlife rescue organisation WIRES arrived to take Mr King Brown Swimmer away to a safer location. It shook us up to think that a snake would come so close to us. They were supposed to be more afraid of us than we were of them! From then on, before every swim we checked the filter and pool for any curled-up slitherers. Fortunately, we never found another swimmer.

Two years later I was a romantically inclined fourteen-year-old. My girlfriends and I all sat together in French class, and we had decided that we all had crushes on frogs (in between our more serious obsessions with Hanson, The

Backstreet Boys and for me—Jonathan Taylor Thomas),
which we insisted on calling by their French name, *grenouilles.*
One day I was on weeding duty in the strawberry patch at
home. On my knees and singing away to myself while pulling
weeds and searching for a stray berry, I heard something
hit a leaf. Excited about the chance to hold a wee *grenouille*
in my hand, I reached over to move back some foliage and
found myself just millimetres away from a brown snake. Time
seemed to stop. It felt as though I was frozen for way too
long, but fortunately the snake didn't move until I had come
to my senses, jumped up and started running. There was
no calm, out-of-body detachment this time: I was shaking,
screaming and crying as I flew into the arms of my mother.
Once she and Dad had calmed me down enough to explain
what had happened, Dad bravely ventured back to the scene
of the crime, where he found nothing. He asked if I could
possibly have mistaken the small thin black irrigation hose
for a serpent, but I knew what I'd seen. I'm still not sure
they entirely believed me, but either way I didn't have to do
any more gardening that day!

Snakes aside, the things that troubled me as I was growing up
were all about being number five in a big family: not enough
new toys; no PlayStation or CD player like my friends had;
having to wear uncool hand-me-down clothes. Being adopted

or looking different from some of my siblings just didn't rate a thought.

I don't remember ever being told that I was adopted and Rani and Damian were too, I just always knew. Once or twice as I got older I let myself have a bit of a joke with people who earnestly enquired, 'So, how old were you when you found out you were adopted?' 'Well,' I answered, 'pretty hard to hide, given my parents are white.' I'd follow up with a 'gotcha' grin.

I know that for some people being adopted is a source of great angst. Not for me. By going to such lengths to bring me into their lives, my parents gave me so much—health, nourishment, education, opportunity and love. Like everyone else who's adopted, I was chosen. There's no such thing as an unplanned adoption. Even later, in my door-slamming teenage years, when many people *dream* of discovering they're adopted, my feelings didn't change. Even then, I was glad to be a Bourke and grateful to my parents for making me one.

I knew we were a bit out of the ordinary: most families didn't have members who were adopted. But then most families also didn't have eight children. Arriving at Mass in an enormous white van was way more irregular to my teenage mind. Being adopted didn't make heads turn each time we traipsed in late; forming two pews' worth all on our own did.

In fact, rather than causing me angst, being adopted made me feel special. I didn't know much about India, but what I did know was that it was a poor country and that whatever life I lived in Australia would be a hundred times better than what I might have had otherwise. Poor Mum made numerous attempts over the years to interest Rani, Damian and me in Indian 'culture', but we just didn't want to know. My view was: I'm Australian, why would I care about that foreign country? Bathurst was a bigger place. People were beginning to ask the dreaded 'where were we from' question. That made me resent them but India too. Mum, however, would always love India.

Not too long after we moved to Forest Grove, my lack of interest in the country of my birth turned into active dislike. Mum had entered a competition in *New Idea* magazine to win a trip for four to India for a week or so. In the entry you had to say why you wanted to go, and Mum wrote that she wanted to see properly as an adult the country that had given her three of her children. With a reason like that, of course she won! She decided to take the eldest, Melissa, then nineteen, who along with Catherine had watched and been part of the adoption process for each of us three, and Rani, thirteen. Damian and I were still just kids and unfussed by it all and Dad had to keep everything running at home, so Mum asked our neighbour and close family friend from Hobbys who had also moved closer to Bathurst, to take the fourth place. Her real name was Hosannah but we all called her Simpy, an abbreviation of her last name. Simpy and Mum had become close friends and she often looked after us kids, especially me when I was the youngest. She had a lot in common with

Mum, including a no-nonsense approach to life, and a love of gardening, the outdoors and animals, and she was thrilled to go on the journey.

Mum came back from India full of stories. Strangely, I don't remember any photos at all, but her words painted a powerful enough picture. She was enraptured by the country, talking animatedly about its people, its chaos, its food, its culture and (surprisingly for Mum, who doesn't like the pastime much) its shopping. However, it was the rest of what she said that had the biggest impact on me. She told us about the masses of beggars they had seen—lame and crippled beggars, child beggars. She told us about the disease-laden water in the taps, and described in graphic detail how ill Simpy had become as a result. She was just telling us what she'd seen, she didn't intend to shock or alarm us. Even so, I was horrified by these accounts in the same way you might be forever freaked out by a campfire horror story you heard at a vulnerable age.

Melissa has always been an extremely emotionally sensitive person. She was hugely affected by the poverty and degradation she'd seen and vowed she would never go back. As to what Rani thought—how she felt about being back in the land she'd come from—as odd and unlikely as it sounds now, we never talked about it. I asked her recently what she remembered of the experience. She spoke positively about the trip. Unlike me, she knows the name of her biological mother and recalled seeing a restaurant of the same name.

I quite liked the painted leaves Mum had brought home from India to hang on the wall. But beyond that, I wanted nothing to do with what I thought of as a gross, impoverished place. Clearly Rani and Damian felt the same way. Life went along as though we'd been born as well as bred in Australia. India just didn't factor. Mum continued to try, though. She'd buy Rani ankle-length Indian patterned skirts which would get hurled to the bottom of her cupboard underneath the mini-skirts. Occasionally Mum would look at us wistfully and ask if she could plait our hair like the Indian ladies did. We refused of course. Books, movies and conversation about India were all received in the same way.

At age nine I finally got the bit of paper that proved what I could have told you anyway: I'm Australian. (As part of the preparation for the trip to India, Rani had already gone through this process so she was able to travel on an Australian passport.) On this particular day, Mum came and picked Damian and me up from school; we went down to the mayor's office, where he put on some strange robes and his big gold mayoral chain and read out something I didn't quite understand, and just like that, we were Australian citizens. He gave Mum the certificates and she dropped us back at school, now 'naturalised'.

A couple of years after Mum's trip, everyone in my class was assigned a major project: to create a poster and an accompanying presentation on a country of our choice. That afternoon, in great excitement, I told Mum all about it. 'What country are you going to choose—India?' she said ever so hopefully. Jeez, I thought to myself, parents are so old. They just don't get anything. 'Nope,' I said. 'America!' I can still see the slight but definite sinking of her shoulders in disappointment.

Mum was already convinced that our brains were being rotted by never-ending consumption of American junk on screen—this just proved it. The terrible unfairness of her opinion was that my parents' strict rules meant I watched less TV than anyone else I knew. In fact, to this day I'm often embarrassed when I'm in a group and everyone laughs at some cryptic pop-culture reference from the 1990s that I just don't get. This ignorance is endlessly embarrassing for someone who lives their life on the internet trying to keep up with memes about the nineties and references to an era that I all but missed.

But what I did get to see, I loved. And my parents' restrictions just made me hungry for more. With so many kids covering such a big age range, there was always someone too young for anything risqué. (When I finished high school, the youngest two, Gabriela and Joseph, were still in primary school.) So the rule was G-rated shows and movies only. Every now and then special dispensation might be made for a PG show if it had some kind of educational aspect, but if it was M-rated, forget it. Long past the age when most of my peers had moved on to *Friends*, *South Park*, *Ally McBeal* and *The*

X-Files, I was still in the land of Pixar and Walt Disney. I had watched *The Lion King* so many times I knew every syllable off by heart, and I still know every song!

There were a few TV shows that got the parental tick of approval and these we kids would watch together. *Full House* and *Saved by the Bell* were my two favourites. The kids in these shows were just like those in the *Sweet Valley High* novels I read over and over: all white teeth and glossy hair. They drove around cool Californian locations in convertibles and wore the latest fashions. I longed to be like them, which usually meant being blonde and blue-eyed. I didn't want that because I was unhappy with my own brown skin, I just wanted the fantasy. I wanted to be coordinated enough to be a cheerleader, too, and able to go on shopping trips with my pals to a gleaming mall. I wanted the whole dreamy package. I didn't know any better. Everything around me served up the American ideal as the ultimate goal.

So I did my project on America, or at least my shallow take on it. To my shame, I scored a D, the first and only time that ever happened. I couldn't work out what had gone wrong, but whatever it was, it was enough to trigger the beginning of the end of my love affair with Uncle Sam—though it would be another two decades before India took its place as the country that would engross me in a far more substantive way than my primitive teenage views of the world ever had allowed.

3

A TASTE OF THE WORLD

Moving in year two from tiny Newbridge Public School to Cathedral Catholic Primary School in the heart of Bathurst proved a mixed bag. On the one hand the school was bigger, which meant there was more to do, more people to meet, and more games to play at recess and 'big lunch'. On the other, it was there that I had my first taste of being bullied.

As well as being deputy principal, Dad was a classroom teacher, and when I reached year five he took my class for the year. He was a great teacher. For downtime he read us *Treasure Island*, complete with excellent pirate voices (unfortunately he caught me out at home reading ahead in an abridged version). His deputy principal role also made him the school's chief disciplinarian, which theoretically meant the mean kids would avoid me like the plague. In practice, it made me a prime target.

It just so happened that the school's biggest troublemaker was in my class. He'd been getting into strife the whole time I'd been there, and no doubt right back to kindy. By year five he had turned his sights on me. There were a few pushes and shoves but he never really physically harmed me. His weapon was social exclusion. He would bully and intimidate the other kids into making sure I was always the last one chosen for team sports and was excluded from games in the playground. Anyone caught being friendly to me would get the same treatment. Even nice, sympathetic kids like the boy in my class I'd tried to befriend at the start of the year backed away for fear of the consequences.

I hated that time. That bully cast such a shadow over my life that I dreaded going to school. But I never told anyone about it. That might seem odd given that Dad was right there, but I didn't want to bring him into it. Most of it was easy for anyone who wasn't looking to overlook— I thought it was my problem to deal with, and I feared making things worse by complaining.

It went on into year six and only came to an end after the nice boy in my class who had been too scared to be my friend felt he could no longer stand back and watch what was going on. He reported it to the principal and the bullying stopped.

I was grateful to him for taking my side, but I also understood why people hadn't done so before. They didn't want to make themselves targets. I didn't blame them for that, but being treated like an outcast made for a very difficult, lonely and emotionally bruising time. I was relieved when I finished primary school and could shake off the bully and make a new start at high school.

But even during those years of being targeted by a bully, I never felt as though I was experiencing racism. He would say mean things as he shoved me out of the line for the bubblers, but I don't recall them being about my background or the colour of my skin. In truth, I've chosen to forget the worst of it, and it's possible there was that kind of undertone to it, but it certainly didn't feel racially motivated. In fact, I seem to have got through my whole early childhood with only one racist insult hurled my way, when a boy at the bus stop called me 'chocolate'. It was such a pathetic attempt that I wondered why he even bothered.

Rani and Damian had copped a bit. Back at Hobbys I remember overhearing Mum and Dad talking about what some kid or other had called them in the playground or on the bus. But unlike me they were extremely popular at school, because of their easygoing natures, generous spirits and athleticism, and any hostility fell away as they made friends with what seemed like the whole of teenage Bathurst. I was the complete opposite: bookish, nerdy, intense, bossy, blunt, and interested in weird stuff like politics, the news and learning the lyrics to *Les Misérables* off by heart.

It had fallen to Melissa to defend Rani and Damian in those very early years at primary school in Blayney, but at Newbridge and later in Bathurst I don't recall there being too many dramas that involved us looking different. Don't get me wrong, there were people who didn't like me, all right, but it was my personality they objected to, not my skin colour. (What did they mean, abrasive and opinionated??)

Or maybe the racism was there and I just didn't see it that way. Where's the line? I've often thought that it's the intent that makes all the difference. All those people who asked me where I was from, *really* from, were they racist? Many people would say yes—the colour of my skin set the tone for them. I personally didn't feel they were being racist, just socially inept, but even so, the more often I was asked that question, the more entrenched my attitude to India became. It was exasperation combined with resentment that turned into loathing—why couldn't people see what I actually was, Australian?

Over the years I came to hate even the word 'India'. It produced a visceral reaction: a physical shudder. I developed a hypersensitive loathing of any associated word too, including 'subcontinent'. I kept this well hidden from most people, but I couldn't hide it from my family. And Melissa, my beloved protector, my 'second mum', wasn't above making use of this knowledge. If she wanted a laugh she would wickedly suggest that I might like to eat some spicy food, then sit back and enjoy the heated reaction it never failed to produce. It was classic sisterly teasing, effective because she knew exactly which buttons to press.

Mum was very big on rolling with the punches, both as a sign of character and as a useful tactic to disarm others. 'No one likes someone who can't laugh at themselves,' she sagely pointed out one day when I decided I was mortally offended at something Damian had said. This was a recurring theme in her motherly advice. A variation, when she thought I was being overly touchy at another of Damian's well-sharpened barbs, was, 'You're not going to get very far in life if you can't laugh at yourself.' There was no point, she told us, in taking on other people's anger. Smiling and moving on was always the better option over getting dragged into pointless arguments. Of course, if someone was picking on one of us, that was different. But in general, smiling at a horn-beeping road-rager was better than angrily honking back, Mum believed. It was a great lesson and one that helped me deal with my later life as a political journalist online. Trolls, flamers—whatever. They had nothing on my brother. I shrugged, chose not to worry and moved on, and sometimes contributed a self-deprecating assessment. I could get angry and upset or choose to laugh or worry. Mum's advice never let me down.

That lesson was for all us kids, but there was another just for Rani, Damian and me. She strongly encouraged us to be the first to make reference to our dark skin. That way, anyone who was contemplating making a racist taunt would realise that it would be an empty and pointless attack. They could only be capable of hurting us if we were sensitive about our skin colour, which we never were.

Her advice certainly seemed to be borne out by experience. Many people claim a 'good sense of humour' as one of their defining qualities. Not me. I know I'm not a funny person—certainly not compared to the rest of my family and particularly my friends. But at high school I found that any time I referred to my skin colour I was guaranteed a laugh. Eliciting mirth from others was such a rarity for me that I kept it up. *You bewdy, I'm onto something here.*

There's no question that I enjoyed being seen as a 'good sport'. But there was always an underlying puzzlement as well. I couldn't figure out *why* people found these references so funny. I never quite grasped that it was because I was acknowledging the elephant in the room. I saw myself as being just like them. Just like within my family, the differences that I saw between me and the people around me were all the regular things that also separated them from one another. Averil had crazy curly hair and was destined to be school captain from the first day of year seven. Rachal was tall, blonde and the one everyone confided in. Amie's Irish genes gave her freckles and a red mane to match. She was gifted musically but hated lessons, whereas I adored English and modern history and read beyond the assigned texts. Our various talents, inclinations, loves, likes and dislikes: these were the things that made us different and dynamic, not the amount of melanin in our skin.

Even though it was okay for me to do it, it was hard to take references to my skin colour from others, and every now and then it got a bit too much. Mum and Dad insisted on us attending a Catholic high school, so off Rani and I went to the all-girls MacKillop College. Typically, the uniforms were designed to be as unflattering as possible, and were made with little regard to the Australian climate. One summer lunchtime I was lying on the grass with three girlfriends, all of us sweltering away in our woollen kilts. We were taking turns to moan about how hot we were when one remarked that I was probably feeling even more uncomfortable than they were, 'because black things attract the heat'. The other two erupted with laughter. I erupted in a different kind of way, storming off in a huff. It was another year before we made up and were properly friends again. We occasionally tease each other about it to this day. Me: 'Remember when you called me black?' Her: 'Remember when you totally cracked the shits and went off like a drama queen?' Mostly we laugh about it. There wasn't any malice behind it, and I knew it.

Another memory, one that still burns, comes from the year we had a big school fundraising fete. While I didn't want anything to do with Indian food, someone clearly did—along with the sausage sizzle and steak sandwiches, the food offerings included a curry stall. I was hanging around with a group of friends at one of the other stalls, hoping that a certain boy, who went to our brother school St Stanislaus College or Stannies as it was known, the first boy I'd ever had a real crush on, would notice me, when I became aware of my name being called over the PA: 'Could Latika Bourke please report to the curry stand.' Students, parents and teachers all had to pitch in for the fete, so I just assumed I was going to be given a small job to do.

When I walked up to the stand, however, I was told no, I wasn't needed there. As I turned away in confusion, I saw my supposed friends standing nearby watching me. They were convulsed with laughter. Even then I didn't get it, and they actually had to explain it to me before I understood they'd just pulled off 'one of the best pranks ever!' They'd humiliated me in front of the whole school and all the parents, and of course the boy of my dreams, for their own amusement. Left to my own devices, it would never have occurred to me that that's what it was about: Latika's Indian, right? A curry-muncher, right? Even though in my head I was as white as they were and I had never eaten a curry in my life!

Humiliation and anger are such physical emotions—it took years before I could recall that incident without feeling a hot rush of blood to my cheeks. Yet even so, I told myself that this feeling was of my own making. I could choose not to be so sensitive. If I let it bother me, it was my own problem. I just needed to shrug, smile and laugh it off, as Mum had said. I thought being able to respond like this was a classically Australian trait: the wonderful ability to readily laugh at yourself. I reminded myself of this over and over.

But for all my resentment at being treated differently because I was brown, I was quite happy to try to pass myself off as black, specifically black American. I no longer worshipped all things from the land of canned cheese, but in my mind, African-American culture was the height of cool. This view was shared by Damian during our teenage years. He led the way, of course, dressing like the black rappers he idolised, while I got my hair braided into tiny plaits, which raised me in the 'cool' stakes at school. Being mistaken for a black American would have been a compliment akin to being perceived as blonde and blue-eyed. That's how I saw it then.

Going outside Australia when I was fourteen broadened my perspective. Mum found the Australian heat unbearable and often spoke longingly of England. When I reached year nine, she and Dad came up with a grand plan to take us overseas to visit some of Mum's relatives whom she hadn't seen since she left Britain more than three decades earlier. My parents were always planning their next great scheme, whether it was setting up a hobby farm, adding another bloody garden bed (that we kids would inevitably have to weed!) to the grounds at Forest Grove, or something more ambitious, like moving the family to the United Kingdom for six months. Rani and Melissa had both moved out of home by this point, but that still left six children, including a toddler. There was (and still is) something crazy, brave and irrepressible about Mum and Dad.

I couldn't wait! How exciting. Never would I have thought we'd be able to fly overseas and actually live abroad. Money was always tight when I was growing up. But somehow Mum and Dad managed to do a lot with very little. They organised a 'home swap', entering our house's availability on an online database of people all around the world who were offering their homes. The best one for us ended up being a place on the border of Wales, hours and hours away from seaside Hythe in Kent where Mum had grown up and where her relatives still lived. Mum, Damian, Dominic, Gabriela, Joseph and I left at the end of the school year in 1999 (Dad and Catherine would follow a few weeks later). The flights, no doubt the cheapest available, went to London via Indonesia and Frankfurt, and we were a ragged, harried bunch when we arrived. I'm not sure how we made it to Heathrow in one piece, but Mum was wise to invest in two Game Boys for us to share on the plane trip over.

It can't have been easy for Mum without Dad for those first few weeks, but by the time Dad and Catherine arrived and Melissa joined us from London, we spent a fun Christmas in a very picturesque country farmhouse, complete with an old Aga stove, in Herefordshire. Hedges lined the road to two huge wooden gates that swung open to a driveway so steep we had to empty the car before tackling the hill. It was terrifying to deal with ice and snow but it all added to the excitement of being so far away from Australia—although weirdly, because of our literary diet of Enid Blyton, the place felt very familiar, almost like coming home. Great big paddocks of scrub were swapped for fields of vivid green, crisscrossed by the hedges I'd read about all my life. The farm no longer had animals, but scattered around the grounds were moss-covered barns and an old stone well.

In the New Year we moved to Dymchurch, closer to Aunty Paddy and Mum's cousins Aecila and her husband David. Here we were just metres from one of the pebble beaches that we'd never quite been able to believe existed when Mum told us about them.

The trip to England was my first taste of the wider world beyond rural New South Wales, and I loved it. The school I went to was co-ed, which was a huge change for me. The kids were different too. In fact, everything was unusual: the accents, the things they did at lunchtime (walked the school perimeter in laps), the curriculum. I wasn't there long enough to make any friendships that lasted beyond our stay, but I felt accepted and liked, and England felt like the sort of country where anyone could fit in.

I got a job babysitting two young children who were neighbours of Aecila and David's in Hythe. The children's parents came home well after the last bus had ambled out of the seaside town, so I would stay over with my relatives. The hours and nights away from my family gave me my first opportunity to expand my sense of self. The money I earned gave me my first taste of independence. I would have been happy to keep living there, but soon the six months was up and we had to return to Bathurst. Back at school I yearned to go back to England and never stopped dreaming of returning.

Roughly coinciding with our return to Australia, I got on the hormonal teen rollercoaster and didn't get off it for a few years. After a brief reprieve from my parents' strict rules about where and with whom we could go out, rules which were easy to enforce living out of town in Bathurst but more difficult in Dymchurch, being stuck back in Forest Grove was a complete downer. I had a fairly torrid relationship with my parents for a while, as a lot of people do at that age. According to them, I was rude, moody, uncommunicative, secretive, lazy and selfish. According to me, they were way too controlling and repressive—I wasn't allowed to go to parties or sleepovers, and they were still trying to exert control over what I watched, listened to and wore. I sank into a self-absorbed funk of loneliness, for which I blamed my parents. I felt trapped and yearned to be my own person again.

We lived too far outside town for me to walk to the shops as I'd done in Dymchurch, and I wasn't allowed to ride my bike in to see friends—the distance was too far and unsafe for a young girl. There was no public transport, so I had almost zero social life outside of school. This was the era before smartphones and instant messaging, and I felt completely isolated. I had one friend whose parents were nearly as strict as mine. During lunch we would glumly sympathise with each other over the fact that yet another party had come and gone without us.

It felt like my only luxury was having my own bedroom, albeit the smallest in the house. It was my retreat, my sanctuary, and I spent most of my time at home in what was dubbed 'the Cave' by the rest of the family, listening to rage-filled rock music and sarcastic Alanis Morissette, reading Sylvia Plath and Annie Proulx and writing mournful poems about my non-existent love life. (I'd moved on from *Sweet Valley High* to literary fiction and especially loved Jane Austen.) When I ran out of other things to do, I studied.

I was desperate for more independence, and when we returned from England I, with the help of Dad, hunted down my first job. I was already interested in journalism, so where else would I go but to the newsagency in town? Dad would pick up his morning paper every day on the way to work and the owners, Geoff and Virginia, happily trained me up in all things from selling lottery and scratchie tickets to crafting balloon arrangements. After a while I left there to join my school friend Jane at Big W, where the longer opening hours allowed me to earn more money.

Walking through the toy aisles one day, I suddenly realised how few dolls there were with non-white skin. Why not I wondered? It wasn't as though Australia wasn't filled with women from all over the world—especially Asia. Where were the Chinese, Japanese, Vietnamese looking dolls. For the first time I asked myself, what if I did have an issue growing up as a brown girl in a white world? When I was still a pre-schooler, Mum had bought me a brown-skinned Cabbage Patch doll with black curly hair, but I realised now that I had never seen another doll that looked like me, or indeed barely anything other than the blue-eyed blonde Barbie standard. Happily, the world has progressed since then. On a recent trip to India one store's major display feature was an Indian Barbie. I laughed and nearly brought one home for Mum. When I was a child, she would have loved nothing more than to make a dark haired contribution to my collection of blonde, blue-eyed Barbies.

I'd been interested in journalism since the early years of primary school. Apparently in year four I took it upon myself to explain to my teacher all about then opposition leader John Hewson's bungle when it came to detailing the prospective goods and services tax. (No wonder I didn't have more friends if all I wanted to talk about was tax policy!) That's not to say I was obsessed with politics at that age. It was a family ritual to sit down together to watch the 6 p.m. local news and then *A Current Affair* (back when Ray Martin hosted the program) before the Sydney news came on, and in the mornings we woke up to Tracy Grimshaw and Steve Liebmann on *Today*, so we all felt quite well informed about things.

I was more interested in the media generally and even fantasised about presenting the travel show *Getaway*. Then when I was twelve it was my job to carry the big black crate full of old editions of the local paper, the *Western Advocate*, down the driveway to leave out for the recycling collection. Reading the top page as I walked along one day, my eye was caught by a story about a young woman who was studying at the local university. The degree was a Bachelor of Arts in Communications—Broadcast Journalism. I didn't need a pen to write it down, it was instantly seared into my memory. That's what I'd do—that journalism degree. Throughout high school my ambition never wavered, and I left school determined to pursue that course. But first I wanted to see a little of the world.

Mum's English birth entitled her biological children (but, unfairly, not Rani, Damian or me!) to a right of abode visa to live and work in England, and Melissa leapt at the opportunity. She was a Princess Diana tragic and was extremely affected by her death (as we all were). Resolved to visit Althorp, Diana's childhood home and now the site of her grave, she set off to London in August 1998. She ended up getting a job as a teacher, and would remain in London for five years in all. She urged me to come over when I left school, and even generously offered to put the cost of my airfare on her credit card until I could pay it off.

I was trying to save, and by year twelve, as well as studying for my Higher School Certificate, I was already juggling two regular jobs (Big W and Muffin Break) plus the odd bit of babysitting for neighbours. Then a new Indian restaurant opened up in Bathurst. Despite having spent my life trying to distance myself from any connection with India, I went there seeking a job. Maybe looking the part would give me an edge over the other applicants, I thought, and if exploiting my supposed 'Indian-ness' would help me get to London sooner, so be it. Sure enough, I landed the job, but the few hours a week I was there set back my relationship with India even further.

The job itself was fine, but the smell of the Indian food seemed to cling to me permanently. It wasn't the first time I'd worked with food—I'd moonlighted in a bakery and donned a ridiculous-looking Muffin Break uniform for a short time to sell toasted sandwiches and warmed muffins—but nothing prepared me for this experience. I would go home at the end of every shift stinking of curry. My hair, which fell to the small of my back, smelled the strongest, but I felt as though the odour had sunk into every pore. Shivering, I would strip down to my underwear outside the house, throw my uniform on the washing line to air it out and then sprint straight to the shower. But no amount of soap and shampoo would remove the smell. I can recall the distinctive odour of butter chicken mixed with Schwarzkopf hair wax even now, and it still nauseates me.

I kept my aversion to Indian food quiet, and the restaurant owners, knowing nothing of it, generously gave me takeaways to bring home. I tried a bit here and there, but the only thing I took to was the innocuous mango lassi. Mum liked Indian food, however, and my school friend Averil loved the leftover curries. Passing on the freebies was really the only upside.

I put up with the job for the last three or four months of year twelve, and then four days after graduation, at the end of 2001, I was out of there. Out of the restaurant, out of school, out of the family home, out of Bathurst, out of Australia. Given my horridness as a teenager, I think Mum and Dad were probably relieved to see me go. Our relationship got better and better once I left home and I could finally do what I wanted to do. At seventeen years and eight months, four months away from legal adulthood, I touched down in London for a year of freedom and exploration.

After all that hard work I should have saved more than I had, but I'd also enjoyed finally being able to buy the things I wanted. Poor Melissa was aghast when I arrived to live with her with just a hundred pounds in my pocket. Luckily, I've never had any trouble finding a job. Initially I temped in a business park in north-west London for a family company that made pita bread and baklava. It was a very boring job—inputting data from customer orders into a computer, in a tiny office of just a few people. The owners were a traditional and very strict Orthodox Christian family. They made my mum and dad look like heathens!

There were many signs the place wasn't for me. On a rare occasion when we all went out as an office group, an older girl, a daughter of the family who owned the company, asked if I liked one of the guys she'd introduced me to that night. 'Sure,' I said. I was very inexperienced in these things: I'd never had a boyfriend, and although I'd formed a few crushes on boys back in Bathurst, they were never reciprocated. It made for great poems! But the conversation took a turn that scared the heck out of me. 'So,' she said, 'you think you could marry him then?' Whoa. If I didn't physically take a step back and put up both palms to ward her off, I sure did mentally.

In the end, the place was far too conservative for a very loud young Australian who'd suddenly been handed her freedom. I was called in one day and advised to look for another job.

I didn't mind. I was keen to make friends and I hadn't found any there.

Within weeks I had found my groove. I landed right in the middle of an excellent gang of warm-hearted Londoners, Linda, Marcel, Joanne, Eddie and Tania, Judith, Sarah and Anju, who took me under their collective wing. Anju's father and uncle owned the business, the unambiguously named VDC—Video Duplicating Company—which turned out videos, CDs and DVDs. They were an Indian family but that never really registered with me. It was completely different to be around them, for starters, they never asked me the dreaded 'where are you from?'. They could so clearly see that I was Australian and not Indian that my 'heritage' was never brought up.

My initial role there was a temp job answering phones. Aussies tend to have a good reputation in England as hard workers and I certainly did my best to add to it. The company kept calling me back in for work, and after a few weeks I landed a permanent role. My job was to look after a group of clients and ensure their CD manufacturing orders progressed on time. This rarely happened, for a range of reasons: equipment would fail, other orders would be prioritised and so on. But my clients were a good bunch who valued communication and organisation over tight delivery deadlines. It was the ideal job for me, suiting my extroversion and anally-retentive organisational skills perfectly. But it was the group of friends

I made there, people I still call friends more than a decade on, that really made England a home for me.

They were all older than me, in their twenties and thirties, but the age difference didn't matter. I preferred hanging out with people I could look up to, learn from and respect. They, in turn, liked to take care of their 'Chicken Tikka', as they affectionately nicknamed me. The subject of India must have come up and somewhere along the line I must have told them I didn't care for Indian food, but the moniker was good-natured and, funnily enough, didn't bother me in the least. VDC was a stopgap for most of us. Marce wanted to be an actor. Linda was a free spirit who was always planning her next adventure, going from scuba diving in Mauritius to some other equally exotic jaunt.

Just like the first time I'd been to England, no one I met ever asked if I was Indian. Because of my accent, everyone knew I was Australian, and that was where they left my identity. I loved the cultural maturity of London. There was so much diversity, so many different British accents belonging to people whose families had come from an amazing range of countries, that a brown-skinned loudmouthed Aussie was the last thing that would appear out of the ordinary.

My first stint in England had begun my process of growing up; now I really spread my wings and started to find my own way. Apart from all the regular things eighteen-year-olds do, like getting their bag stolen at a club in Soho, trying their first cigarette (bumming a puff and exhaling quickly), navigating the night bus home because they stayed out later than the last train and couldn't afford a cab, and getting blind drunk at the pub then pretending to their sister that the reason they're ill is because they ate a bad pizza as opposed to too many Bacardis, I learned above all things the importance of enjoying my own company.

I lived from pay cheque to monthly pay cheque, and often by the end of the third week had little money left to do anything. At times I had to risk fare evasion fines on the Tube because I couldn't afford the monthly travel card. But London is a city where you can do a lot with nothing. I took myself off to visit the Imperial War Museum, where all my modern history lessons came alive. I went to galleries and looked around shopping centres and saw the sights. I didn't need money to absorb this city.

If I could have I would have stayed in London forever. But I was wearing out my welcome with Melissa, who had put up with her eighteen-going-on-thirty-year-old sister living on the couch in her one-bedroom flat for a year. On top of that, my two-year working visa said I could only work for half that time. So home I must go to pursue my dream of journalism.

When it was time for me to leave, the wonderful VDC crew showered me with gifts, including a photo album full of treasured memories of our riotous nights out and a notebook filled with handwritten inscriptions urging me on to my goal.

I wept a good deal on the plane home. Quietly, of course, the way I'd been raised, not making a fuss. I didn't want to leave behind my wonderful new friends, or Melissa, or the excitement and endless options in London. I dreaded returning to boring old Bathurst. But I knew what I wanted. I was going to be a journalist. And as I told everyone at VDC, I wanted to be one of the best in my field when I got back to Australia. And if that meant returning to my hometown, so be it. I had a goal to reach and a task to achieve. But as it happened, the Communications course at Bathurst's Charles Sturt University was widely regarded as the best in Australia.

4

NEWSHOUND HAS *SLUMDOG* EPIPHANY

Life was dreary when I returned home. Away from the energy and excitement of London's bright lights, I began to suffer from what I called Small Town Syndrome, where the lack of choice and options felt claustrophobic. I stayed with Mum and Dad for about a week or so, then Mum (somewhat eagerly!) helped me find my first solo home—a very small bedsit at the end of Keppel Street in Bathurst that overlooked the historic railway station and cost seventy-five dollars a week in rent. It was small, but it was mine and it was perfect. I splashed out on a tiny bar fridge but bought everything else second-hand, except my bed from home. Unlike Rani, Catherine and Melissa, I had refused to learn to cook for the family when Mum was out tutoring and Dad was still at work. Somehow I got away with it. But it meant a good six months living on bacon sandwiches and bowls of Nutri-Grain before I got fed up and taught myself to cook from *Good Taste* magazines.

Before I left for England I had applied for and received a place at Charles Sturt University, deferring my start date for a year, so there were no worries on that front. I resumed my old job at Big W, got another job pulling beers and serving grilled meat plates at the Victoria Hotel over the road from my flat, and prepared for university life.

Of my old school friends only Amie and Jane were still living in Bathurst; Rachal and Averil had moved to Sydney and Wollongong respectively to study. Jane moved into my building, taking the flat underneath me. We were so close that she gave me a set of keys so I could use her washing machine, which was a little awkward when I once entered without warning at, ahem, an inconvenient time for her and her boyfriend who weren't properly dressed for company.

I'd been so keen to get started at uni, but by the end of the first semester I was already feeling disillusioned. There was a lot of defining, analysing and dissecting of the media but not much practising for the job itself. I became impatient. I wanted to do, not talk about it. Charles Sturt University in Bathurst is renowned for having one of Australia's best communications courses. Having it on my CV helped, but I was always impatiently wanting to do more. On the few occasions when we got to do practical work, we took turns practising reading from an autocue to camera in a mock studio. It felt natural and exciting, like an intelligent performance.

I knew that I wanted to have a serious go at presenting in some form. Reluctant to wait, I took myself down to 2BS Gold, a greatest hits station aimed at an older audience, housed on one of Bathurst's main streets. I explained to the receptionist what I was about and, acting more confident than I felt, asked to see the manager. I was in luck. Phil Cole was a decent guy who was always on the lookout for keen students. He was backed by the station's owners, Ron and Stephanie Camplin, who supported his efforts to give keen up-and-comers a go behind the mic.

It started off as unpaid work experience, which my lecturers encouraged and praised. I showed up for a few hours each Tuesday afternoon, trying to prove that I was reliable and enthusiastic. I began by writing local news stories and 'cutting grabs' (isolating a short snippet, usually no more than seventeen seconds which helps explain the story the newsreader has presented), which meant I needed to learn how to use the audio editing software. I was already a gadget geek—I'd been the first in my high school to buy a mobile phone (that was where some of my hard-earned money had gone), a clunky old Philips Savvy that initially didn't even receive text messages—so that part was easy.

There was only one other student on my course who had thought to do the same thing (another Bathurst local, as it happened). I was astonished that none of the other students in my class realised what rich pickings 2BS was. In between the familiar tunes from The Beatles, The Hollies, Elvis Presley and Michael Bublé and the odd couple of hours of chat, they ran local news bulletins. Eventually Phil Cole trusted me enough to let me write and read some of these bulletins. What I turned out were hideously clunky six-paragraph obscenities that would have got me laughed out of almost any major newsroom. (A typical radio news story is two sentences and then a 'throw' to the 'soundbite', or snippet, from whoever is commenting on the story to make it news.) My reading was no better than my writing. Somewhere I have a CD of my first-ever news read on-air. My voice sounds thin, shaky and childish. It wasn't as easy when you were broadcasting to a real-life audience and not just mucking around with your classmates. The poor listeners of Bathurst!

But Phil could see potential in me; along with the morning host and other key people at the station, he kept helping me develop my skills until, after a few months, he gave me my first paid media job. I thought all my Christmases had come at once, even though it was just presenting a hokey Saturday morning show—local buy, swap and sell announcing. But it was perfect, just the foot in the door I needed. At first I couldn't afford a car and didn't know how to drive so I had to walk the several blocks between my flat and the studio on George Street to be on-air at 6 a.m. In winter, the entire town would be enveloped in mist. I slept in my trackies the night before and abandoned the warmth of my doona only at the very last possible minute.

I stayed on at uni, but by second year all I really wanted to do was work. Lectures and tutorials were far too much talk, too much theory and not enough practice. As seems to be my default setting in life, I continued to burn the candle at both ends. Mornings were spent trudging to and then enduring uni. Afternoons were spent either at Big W (which I stuck with until my radio job gave me enough hours) or at 2BS and then the gym. I had an established ritual for the evening, watching every TV news bulletin, beginning with the five o'clock news on Ten and finishing with *The 7.30 Report* with Kerry O'Brien, and then staying up for *Lateline* on the ABC.

In May, I curled up under doonas, too poor to turn on the heater—saving the dollars for when the cold really bit in June—to watch the federal budget. And I made up an excuse for running late to meet Amie when one of our regular Saturday evening catch-ups happened to fall on 2004 election night and I secretly hung back to see the result.

On weekends, I would shout myself the papers and breakfast at Elie's Cafe or Zieglers and bags a giant table for a few hours while I devoured my French toast, maple syrup and bacon, and—more importantly—the 'long reads' in Saturday's

Sydney Morning Herald. I cut out news story ideas I could mimic or flesh out with a local angle. I couldn't pass a broken window in a store on the main street without ringing up the owner to find out if there was a story behind it. I was a hound, always on the hunt, no matter how small the field.

After overdoing it in London, when I got back I gave up alcohol for two years. Amie hated drinking but we both loved dancing, something we had enough confidence to do completely sober, so our nights out together were spent at either the Eddy or the Ox, just a block apart from each other. It was at the Ox that I met my first boyfriend, Jason, who deejayed there by night. We dated for a year or two before realising we were much better as good friends, which we remain to this day.

I turned up on campus and did my assignments and got good marks in the subjects I liked and passed the ones I didn't, but the majority of my energies were spent on my radio job. Just being in Bathurst was a chore after London. My uni classmates were having a great time pub-crawling through Bathurst but I rarely joined in. I was well and truly over small-town life. I had loved growing up in the country but after twenty years it was time to expand in ways my hometown couldn't offer.

In my third year I was finishing off my degree while hosting the morning show from nine till twelve Monday to Friday. I got away with it because the job was technically part-time. It was a tremendous opportunity. Even back then very few country radio stations in Australia could afford to run their own local programming at that time of day; most (now including 2BS) would syndicate a big-name program from the state capital. I got there just at the right time, and made the most of the opportunity I'd been given.

At the beginning of 2006, as a newly minted graduate, I landed a job at the 2UE radio newsroom in St Leonards on Sydney's lower north shore. Looking back, I was hugely underqualified for this giant step up from the airwaves of Bathurst, but they threw me a bone and I chomped and chomped and chomped.

I love being a journo, but it is much less glamorous than people assume. The newsroom had a mix of journalists: old hands like Steve Blanda who'd been reading the news for decades and the then breakfast news editor Derek Peterson— who is still one of the country's finest radio news writers. He was a master and generously taught all the newcomers how to craft a news script so that each word packed meaning into the thirty seconds or so you had to tell the story. Others were up and comers in the prized state politics, courts or police rounds but no less dedicated or talented. Then there were those, like me, who were still wet behind the ears. With this huge mix of talent and experience at hand, it was a great place to learn. The first task was to hone my news-writing skills and polish my presentation, learning to conquer the nervous rush that overcame me whenever I hit the 'on-air' button. And trust me, those nerves more than tripled when I knew I was speaking to an audience in the big smoke!

Although I was thrilled to be back in a city, I was working hard for not much money. I also discovered that Sydney is an expensive city in which to live by yourself, which I did even though most of my family was also now in Sydney.

Catherine's cystic fibrosis had seen her spending more days in Sydney's Westmead Hospital than she did at home in Bathurst, and the travel became exhausting for Mum. My parents had decided to move so they could be closer to Westmead (and, after Catherine's double lung transplant in 2004, St Vincent's Hospital in inner-city Darlinghurst) and to provide more schooling and university options for the younger kids, who were all proving to be musically talented and incredibly gifted (Joe skipped a year of school). While I was still at uni, they had moved to a leafy suburb in the Hills District, not too far from where Dad grew up and where he and Mum had lived in the early years of their marriage. At the time, Damian and I both had our own places in Bathurst, and Melissa was still in London, but Catherine, Dominic, Gabriela and Joe made the move over the Dividing Range with Mum and Dad. Now that I was in Sydney too, it was nice to have them relatively close, but I needed to live much nearer to work, and besides, I was well used to having my own independent space by now, so moving 'home' wasn't an option.

As a newsroom junior-burger I was part of the 'pool' whose lives were dictated by a rolling roster of shifts—overnights, breakfasts and weekends. One week you'd finish at 4 a.m., the next week you'd be getting up at that time to work the breakfast shift. Daytime on-the-road reporting shifts were as prized as they were rare.

Once more I was getting by pay cheque to pay cheque, but this time there was no Melissa to be my safety net. I was living by myself in a one-bedroom flat above St Leonards train station. The flat was infested with cockroaches and looked directly into a row of offices, but it was modern and it was mine. Rent was initially $320 a week, which was substantially more than half of what I was bringing home. I could already barely afford to live, but during my two-year stint in the harbour city the rental crisis took hold, which sent my rent soaring to $380 and then some.

Living alone was an indulgence I clung to as long as possible. After so many years living in a large family, taking two-minute showers because we were on tank water in the middle of the drought, and never being quite sure who'd been in my room riffling through my stuff, I valued my independence over everything. But when my rent ticked over the $400 mark, I had to concede defeat. I moved into a share house up the road in Greenwich, even closer to the 2UE office. It took me years to pay off the credit card bills I racked up during that time. I've never had a credit card since.

At the station, the lower you were on the ladder, the more overnight shifts you got—'mid–dawn' (midnight to dawn), as they were known. I got a lot of these. We all grumbled about them, but truth be told, as long as I got enough sleep during the day I didn't actually mind them, at least at first. There was a bank of TV monitors where I could flick between broadcasts, and between 1 and 4 a.m. generally the only new news was that on the international channels, BBC, CNN and UK Sky. They were full of international stories, and I absorbed as much as my drowsy brain would allow. I didn't yet own an iPod (let alone a smartphone) on which I could listen to podcasts. In fact, I couldn't even afford my own internet connection at home. So I loved having the newsroom to myself and being able to pump the latest BBC feed through the speakers for hours.

In time I moved up the ladder a bit and began to be sent out on assignment to cover stories. My very first on-the-road 'job' makes me chuckle to this day, especially when younger journos ask me about my early years in the industry. I was despatched to the Sea Life Sydney Aquarium to cover the hard-hitting news of a new turtle's arrival. I diligently and earnestly wrote up my forty-second 'script' for a 'vox' or 'voicer' (a report where the newsreader reads the introduction or lead then plays your voiced-up radio report) and filed it over the phone back to the St Leonards mothership. On my way back to work I asked the taxi driver to turn on the radio so I could hear my story. Alas, it never got a run. I was crestfallen.

As I later learned, it was never meant to be aired. It was always intended to be a practice run to get me to learn very basic but crucial aspects of being on the road, such as calling a taxi in plenty of time and collecting natural sound (like the splash of the turtle entering the water, which I failed to record). It was about learning how to file in plenty of time before the 'top of the hour' or the next news bulletin (filing by a quarter to the hour was the ideal). It was about learning to quickly isolate grabs, in those days using portable cassette players, and after finding a nice quiet place, to file the grabs back to the newsroom by holding the mobile phone next to the speaker as the audio snippet played.

In 2007 and 2008, I covered a mix of news around the city, from the courts to New South Wales Parliament House in Macquarie Street, from sports training sessions to the latest police sting. All this practice meant that when I finally got to go to the big jobs, such as covering a lunch address by Prime Minister John Howard in Sydney's Ryde, I was properly prepared to file back to the newsroom his latest comment on the interest rate rise which derailed his election campaign.

But I wasn't always prepared. I made one of the biggest mistakes of my career on the road for 2UE. I was reporting on a court case involving young Sydney woman Lauren Huxley, who'd been violently attacked and left for dead in her own home. Her older sister, Simone, was reading out a victim impact statement, which was written in first person, and I mistook Simone for Lauren herself. I breathlessly reported this back and went live on air with the latest update. Then, to my horror, as I sat back down in the media section of the court-room, all the other journos' phones began flashing up with messages asking why they hadn't reported this development.

It was one of the worst moments in my life. I had embar-rassed my station and, worse, potentially added to the grief and anguish of a family who had already suffered so much. The Huxleys were incredibly gracious and accepted my and the station's apology without any hesitation. Still, I felt sick with worry that my actions might have caused them further pain. Professionally I was humiliated, and that night I cried myself to sleep, hating myself for my error and wondering if I had the guts to show my face in the newsroom the next day. Of course, as is the case in life, things are never as bad after a night's sleep, and I did what anyone would do—got on with it. But I was shaken by the blunder. That's the flipside of working in the media. When you do well it's public and everyone congratulates you, but when you fail everyone is there to watch you, and your mistake can have dreadful consequences.

Determined to do better, I redoubled my efforts, and began volunteering to do extra, unpaid shifts so I could sharpen my filing skills from the road. My English mates had passed on to me their love of 'roundball football' (soccer), and I started to cover Sydney FC's training sessions and games for fun. It was a dual win in my eyes. I got to watch games for free and give the burgeoning A-League additional media coverage.

I wasn't alone in putting up my hand for extra shifts. Other journalists in the newsroom would also offer to work on their days off if they were following a particular case through an inquest or the courts. It was sometimes the only way to break free from reading the 2 a.m. news to what felt like no one.

One weekend in 2008, I was working a late shift in the 2UE newsroom when one of my colleagues, Matt de Groot, arrived for work bursting to tell me about an amazing film he had just seen, *Slumdog Millionaire*. The reason he was so fired up was that the lead female character was called Latika, a name he'd never heard before meeting me. Actually, Matt was the second person to try to tell me about it. One other friend had started to talk about the film, but I quickly established that it was about India and after that I didn't want to hear any more. I dismissed it. However, *Slumdog* had gone on to become a box office sensation, and soon it felt like everyone had seen it.

My exposure to international news had nurtured my existing passion for politics and world affairs (SBS news was my favourite of the five television channels' evening broadcasts), and as part of this, India had begun to intrigue me, but only in a geopolitical sense. Thinking about Australia's strategic interests, I was often puzzled as to why there was so much focus on our relationship with China but not on India. But beyond that, my attitude towards the country of my birth hadn't softened. In fact, just the opposite. I still hated any attempt to link me to India, so when people I knew started raving to me about *Slumdog*, saying 'You have to see it,' I dug in my heels. The more people told me I *had to*, the more obstinately I refused.

It was going to be impossible to avoid, however. So this time I gave in and let Matt tell me all about it—or at least I pretended to listen. Secretly I switched off. I didn't want to hear about something that people might use as a way of connecting me to a country that I was still insisting had nothing to do with me. I had spent so much time having to deny that I was anything but Australian to all the Rude Inquisitors, and now this film had come along to disrupt all that.

By the end of 2008, I had begun to grow impatient with the overnight shifts and crumbs of on-the-road assignments that had to be shared between too many newshounds in the newsroom. I hadn't minded overnights to begin with, but now the odd hours threw my body out of whack. I asked my boss for a better deal. In response I got the tiniest of pay rises but no change to my shifts. Regular hours were an absolute luxury in the newsroom and not one that was about to be thrown my way. While there were benefits to being a general reporter covering a range of news stories, homelessness, charity appeals, the latest economic data and the like, it was ad hoc. I wanted something substantial to plough into. Without some sort of regularity, the crazy hours and thrifty lifestyle were beginning to outweigh the positives. With no hope in sight and facing years of life in the pool, I began to explore the idea of leaving journalism altogether.

So I went and got a passport. Not to travel. I wasn't going anywhere; I could barely afford the passport fee, let alone an airfare. No, I decided that if I was never going to be able to afford to travel on my own dime I might as well apply to be a flight attendant. I registered with Virgin and Qantas and made it through the initial application processes. Then I was called back to a group trial where we had to take part in mock customer-service scenarios and fill in personality tests.

I must have flunked the tests, because that was as far as I got. Which was fortunate, really. Late in 2008, a junior role came up in the Canberra press gallery for 2UE and its sister Fairfax radio stations around the country—3AW in Melbourne, 4BC in Brisbane and 6PR in Perth. My boss was very supportive of me and keen to give me a break; when this posting came up he offered it to me straight away. I had loved politics from an early age. So much so that I hadn't realised it was odd to be asking my high school teacher about the French nuclear tests at Moruroa Atoll. I remember as a young teenager eavesdropping on a discussion between two year twelve girls at the sports carnival about Keating and Hawke's economic legacy ('too much debt!') and thinking that was the sort of conversation I wanted to be having, and understanding. This incredible opportunity to report on politics from the nation's capital was a dream come true.

A few weeks later I was driving down the Hume Highway, looking forward to the prospect of long but regular hours (no more night shifts!) and a substantial pay rise. And sure enough, it would soon turn out to be a great move. Pretty soon, strings of professional breakfast, lunch, dinner and drinks dates would fill my diary. Socialising changed from dancing away empty nights in Sydney clubs to discussing the ways of the world with all sorts of politicians with vastly different ideas and solutions. As it happened, Australian politics was about to undergo a tumultuous upheaval and I had a front row seat.

Joining the press gallery would prove to be a defining career move, but at first I was miserable. It took me about six months to adjust to living in Canberra. The capital's climate was the same as Bathurst's—hot summers and bracingly cold winters with foggy mornings but cool, clear days. After London and Sydney, the city's pace also felt far too similar to Bathurst's. Restaurants and bars closed early and didn't bother opening at all on Sundays.

I moved into a flat with a Fairfax photographer, Glen McCurtayne who became an immediate friend, introducing me to his own mates and colleagues in the gallery. I'd met him while covering Kevin Rudd's successful 2007 election campaign. We hosted a few parties here and there, but I initially missed Sydney's nightclubs enough to find myself back on the Hume Highway every Friday night. But that habit petered out as I became more and more absorbed by the political world around me—what some might unkindly call 'the bubble'.

There were plenty of things Canberra would never provide, but I realised it was unfair to compare it to anywhere else. Eventually I began to see its better points. Clean air, no tolls and little traffic made a big difference. But most of all I loved living in a city bursting with intelligent people. There were few other places in Australia where you could go to a bar, meet a perfect stranger and end up talking about D.K. Rangnekar's book *The Politics of Poverty* for the night. It might sound wanky, nerdy or even dull to those who don't share my passion, but I found it energising.

The press gallery, for the most part, was surprisingly collegiate, and far less competitive than the Sydney media set. Some of the old-timers had worked in the red-carpeted corridor on the Senate's second floor of Parliament House for decades. Once I'd been there for a while, I realised what a small place it was. Friendships crossed media lines, and some of the gallery were married to or dating producers, cameramen or other journalists from rival outlets. There was still competition, of course—everyone wants to get the scoop—but it was a place where you could make genuine and lasting friendships. It felt as though I had finally found my place in life.

Even better, once I started making contacts and getting a real insight into what was going on in the corridors of Parliament (in other words, all the things powerbrokers pretend are not happening when they're speaking publicly), I found the place and my new role completely intoxicating. Like any other job it had its downsides, but for the most part I woke to the sound of the news theme on the radio alarm, ready to jump out of bed and start my day.

Within a year of my move to Canberra, one of the most gripping episodes in Australian politics began to unfold. It would set the course for three different leaders, and we're still feeling the effects years later. The Liberal Party and its coalition partner the National Party, then in opposition, were on the cusp of splitting for good over the issue of whether or not to support an emissions trading scheme to price carbon pollution. Not only did I have a front row seat from which to observe these events play out, at times I even had backstage access. I had some excellent sources who were telling me just how doomed was the hold of Liberal leader Malcolm Turnbull (who supported an emissions trading scheme) on the job. But I worked for a radio station that few people in the capital were able to tune into (keep in mind that radio streaming apps were only just being introduced). While I could keep the good listeners of 2UE and 3AW and the rest informed, there was no immediate way of communicating the information I was receiving to the rest of the press gallery, or to the 'players' inside Parliament House.

So I turned to Twitter. I had joined the microblogging site in March 2009 on one of my many Saturdays back in Sydney. My ex-2UE colleague Alison Piotrowski had encouraged me to sign up. 'Kevin Rudd's on it,' she told me, knowing exactly the right recruitment trick. Well, I had an obligation to know what the prime minister was saying, so I joined. My first tweet was hardly illustrious: 'Bought figs from Kingston market,' I solemnly informed my few dozen followers.

But when I started tweeting about federal politics, as at this time only a few in the gallery were, my followers ballooned into the hundreds, then the thousands and eventually the tens of thousands. No one told me to do it. It just seemed like the sensible thing to do. I needed to talk to the political 'beltway' and I needed to make them listen. And listen they did. It became clear that Twitter was a text version of what radio had always provided, instant, up-to-the-minute—sometimes up-to-the-second—news that people craved when situations were changing quickly. The difference was that a tweet was written, tangible and shareable, and unlike radio, it was something you could easily go back and locate if you missed the top-of-the-hour news broadcast.

Turnbull's leadership did indeed come to an end after months of warning signs, played out through media coverage, topped with a savage final fortnight when the coalition nearly tore itself apart over climate change policy. Those two weeks at the end of 2009 were to be more far-reaching than anyone— the media, the politicians or the public—realised at the time. Politically, these events were a foreshadowing of how diabolical climate policy would be for other leaders, including Labor prime ministers Kevin Rudd and Julia Gillard.

They also created a new frontier for reporting. A well-informed tweet sent just minutes before a critical party room meeting could make as many waves as a front-page newspaper story. Some politicians were quicker to realise the potential than others. Most tried it for themselves but only the brave tended to stay on—publically at least. Privately, most MPs and senators, not to mention their staffers, are quietly hooked into the Twitter drip feed of politics. I am constantly amazed by the number of politicians who will open a conversation about a photo of my cats that I may have tweeted, or a new television show I have started watching! As consumers themselves, most politicians understood the value of news reported via social media and would respond to it in the ways they might any other news report. Contacting the journalist, informing, elaborating and yes, often spinning with the hope of swaying the way the news was being told according to their world view. By the year's end, we journalists were heading into an election year with a new benchmark for deadlines: *now*. It was frenzied stuff. During this period, fourteen-hour days became the norm. 'Spare time' was spent having dinners with contacts and sometimes filing afterwards for the 9 and 10 p.m. bulletins and influential breakfast bulletins.

Of course, this all meant I had little time for romance. I'd had just the one boyfriend in Bathurst. I had met two people I could have been serious with in Sydney, but to my great sorrow they didn't feel the same way about me. As I tried to get over them, I went on plenty of dates, but they were usually one-offs that ended lamely—with me faking emergency phone calls from friends, for instance, followed by watching *Bridget Jones's Diary* on my couch alone with a tub of ice cream.

I can laugh about them now, but I can still hardly believe how some of those dates turned out. One time, a fellow I met at a bar in Sydney asked me out for lunch. I should have known at the time that something was suss. He refused to give me his number, and when he phoned me the number was blocked. Over the meal, while discussing a mutual love of soccer, I jokingly said I could always google his district team results if he refused to tell me. 'But how do you know the name I've given you is my real name?' he said seriously. Too seriously.

'You're joking, right? Your name is John, isn't it?' I asked. He didn't confirm it. Oh my God, I thought, his name isn't John. Who the hell is he and what on earth am I doing having lunch with someone who won't tell me their real name? I'd had so many awful dates by then that I wasn't even horrified. Instead I chose to seize the moment. I'd always wanted to walk out on a date in dramatic circumstances. I stood up, hailed a cab, and left him to finish both our meals and pay the bill.

Some encounters turned out better than that one but there were still no common interests that offered hope of anything ongoing. However, one date in Canberra proved to be life-changing. Not romantically. In fact, if there had been any romantic chemistry I might never have had my epiphany. I met him to share some Chinese food, but it was clear that the salt and pepper prawns were quickly turning out to be the highlight of the evening. Straining for conversation, my date—let's call him Tim—suggested we go back to his place and watch a DVD.

Even though I knew the date was going nowhere, it was still only about eight o'clock. I had been so unsuccessful in my romantic life that I was trying to be as open-minded as possible, worried that I was being too fussy. I didn't need George Clooney, just someone—preferably someone smarter than me—who would enjoy talking about the same things as I did (mostly news and politics) and have as much to bring to the conversation. Anyway, I accepted Tim's offer.

When we got to his place, Tim suggested we watch *Slumdog Millionaire*, his latest addition to his DVD collection. I wasn't about to go off on my usual spiel, so I pressed my internal mute button and agreed.

It was only the second film I'd seen that was set in India. The other was *City of Joy*, one of the rare exceptions to my parents' 'G-rated movies only' rule. A few months after its cinema release in mid-1992, Mum rented it from the video store. The five of us older children sat down with our parents to watch it. Even though it was rated M for 'low-level violence', Mum was excited for us to see it, so Damian and I in particular could understand 'what India's really like!'

Directed by Roland Joffé of *The Killing Fields* fame, *City of Joy* employed the old strategy of featuring a (then) big Hollywood star—Patrick Swayze—to draw audiences into a downbeat story; in this case, life in an Indian slum. Om Puri plays a farmer forced to leave his land and move to Calcutta (as Kolkata was known then) with his family. Tricked and cheated, they fall further and further through the cracks until he finds work as a rickshaw driver. He forms a bond with the Swayze character, a disillusioned American doctor, and shows him that there is hope even among the poorest of the poor.

To be honest, I had to look it up in order to describe it: all I can remember about it is rickshaws and rain—that, and the fact that Mum and my older sisters thought Swayze was pretty damn hot. (I was too young to share such an assessment, although a few years later when I saw *Dirty Dancing* it was a different matter!) Puri's character is actually from Bihar, just like Damian and me, but I remembered none of his story. I don't blame myself or my attitudes to India for this. I was just a kid, not even ten, and in spite of Mum's best efforts, India just wasn't something that figured in our lives. We didn't see ourselves as anything but Happy Little Australians. The film didn't have the revelatory effect Mum had been hoping for, but nearly two decades later, *Slumdog Millionaire* certainly did.

It opens with a scene that helped earn it an MA rating for 'strong themes and violence': the hero, Jamal, being hideously tortured. This boy from the slums of Mumbai is on the brink of winning the jackpot on India's version of *Who Wants to Be a Millionaire*, and because the accepted wisdom is that poor must equal idiot, he is believed to be cheating. It's the police doing the torturing in an attempt to make him confess. Through a series of flashbacks, Jamal relates the incidents in his past that have taught him each correct answer.

This initial scene was a real turn-off for me: yet more of the movie violence that causes me to wince and avert my eyes, I thought. But six minutes and twenty seconds in, the first of director Danny Boyle's trademark montages begins. We are taken into the life of a tiny Jamal and his brother and friends as a game of cricket on private land leads to a police chase that winds through the streets to the slum that is his home. It's impossible to exaggerate the effect this scene had on me. Jolted to attention, I stared at the screen amazed. 'Holy hell, *that's* what it's like, that's what Mum was on about, that's what I could have been?' I forgot to breathe. I was tingling all over. I wanted to drink in every tiny detail in every frame.

Twenty-two minutes into the film and this time it was a sound that caught me: Jamal invites another street child, a girl, to join him and his brother in their very own version of the Three Musketeers. The girl introduces herself—'I'm Latika'. Naturally she pronounces it in the correct Indian way, LAT-ika, rather than the version I'm used to, La-TEEK-a. Despite detesting India, I always loved my name. I liked that it was unusual. Nobody else I knew had it (I was well into my teens before I even heard of another girl called Latika), and everyone liked it. Now suddenly there was this other 'me'. After years spent not even bothering to look at the name key rings and mugs in souvenir shops because I knew mine would never be there between the Kellys and Marias, hearing my name 'normalised' unlocked feelings I didn't know I had.

My tears started and did not stop. A few scenes later, the men who had 'rescued' the slum children started burning out the eyes of those with the best singing voices so they would be more pitiful and thus earn more money on the streets. By now I had graduated to heaving sobs, and I could hear Mum in my head telling me about all the child beggars she had seen who had been deliberately harmed in just this way. But sitting in Tim's lounge room, I kept all this to myself. It was all too personal and profound to share with a virtual stranger.

From Tim's point of view, no doubt I was just another girl crying at a movie.

For years I had pushed away everything Mum had told me on her return from India about the lives of children there, and particularly all the implications about what my life might have been like had I not been adopted. It was much easier to focus on the belief that I was fated, destined to be a Bourke, brought up in Australia. That way I didn't have to think about the fate I had avoided—the fate shared by so many Indian children born into poverty—and feel guilty that I had somehow escaped, feel guilty about what could have been. Now, in a few minutes, *Slumdog* had broken down the walls I had spent years building up. For the first time I allowed myself to imagine what sort of life I might have led. If I hadn't been taken to the orphanage, would I have been a 'slumdog' too?

Over its two-hour running time, *Slumdog Millionaire* yanked me out of my deliberate blindness, smashing open my insecurities and my prejudices; it left me filled with sadness and shame that I had refused for so long to acknowledge this part of myself. As the end credits rolled, I knew that I had started to let India into my heart and that nothing would ever be quite the same.

Something inside me was telling me that I had to go to India, that I had a duty, an obligation to see this country for myself. It was waiting for me, I felt. All of a sudden my existing sense of myself, the prized details that had always made up my identity, seemed tiny and inconsequential in the context of this place where my life had begun. India was a part of me. And just as I would one day show my partner my old schools and home in Bathurst, I felt I needed to show myself my origins too. It wasn't about filling an empty space inside myself. I didn't feel incomplete. Nor did I feel there was some unexplainable aspect about myself I had to discover. It was just an understanding that life hadn't begun at eight months and I was just a link in a much greater chain. Even completing medical questionnaires or answering doctors' questions about whether there was a history of some condition in my family and having to say, 'No idea. I'm adopted,' had never bothered me. This feeling wasn't about me, it was about India. It demanded to be known. It was no longer a question of whether I wanted to identify myself as having been born in India. I had been. And now I had to act on it, because I had started to see what could have been me.

But things weren't so simple. *Slumdog* had changed my outlook, but I was still terrified at the idea of confronting the reality of India. Over the years I had heard countless times about the 'amazing', 'profound' effect India had on westerners who went there. That had been the case at least since The Beatles travelled there in the 1960s, but it seemed to have become more fashionable than ever through the 1990s and into the new century. I didn't want to be one of those westerners who went and discovered themselves in India and came back suddenly loving Bollywood and Buddhism. Even Alanis Morissette, my favourite singer for so long, had found the country 'life-changing'. That scared the hell out of me. I didn't want my life to change.

I was in my twenties, happily partying and socialising; and expanding my contact directory. Building my career and working hard were my priorities. I liked my life and found it rewarding. Things were good, too good to risk any disruption.

5

A TIME OF GREAT AND GRADUAL CHANGE

The internal struggle between my newfound feelings about India and my unwillingness to uproot my world continued. I let the idea of going to India percolate for the best part of 2010. There was a lot going on, and opening up to the thought of travelling to the country of my birth was just one part of it.

It was a formative year for me in so many ways. As a radio journalist I had been trained to work towards the 'top of the hour', but the demand for news was now instant, by the minute or the next tweet. I was doing what felt like several jobs in one, live tweeting, filing for radio and networking with contacts trying to find stories I could break. And I loved it. It was gruelling, intense but fulfilling and interesting. The political landscape was evolving drastically, and then the Labor Party made a seismic shift that caught us all by surprise.

On the night of 23 June I was in Sydney attending the Walkley Young Journalist of the Year awards. I was still plagued by credit card debt thanks to my years living in Sydney on a baby journalist wage. No matter how hard I tried to pay it off, the debt seemed to creep back up. I needed five thousand dollars to clear the rest of my debt once and for all, and the Walkley Foundation's award for the Young Journalist of the Year was offering not only a trip to see the BBC in London and CNN in New York but also five thousand dollars in cash. I had taken it as a sign to enter.

I always laugh at being called a 'pioneer' of using social media for journalism. It's not true. There were other journalists on Twitter long before I joined. My own use just happened to coincide with a rapid take up of the medium by readers and journalists and a major story in the leadership spill that developed faster than the media could keep up. This was before the launch of a free to air rolling news channel in Australia and live blogging on online news sites was still rare. I had joined Twitter grudgingly, and only began using it because the 2UE and 3AW news bulletins, although widely listened to in Sydney and Melbourne, were missed by that vital political class in Canberra. But to try something new I needed the equipment. Tweeting was an optional extra back then. Now, many newsrooms actively seek social media skills, and they equip and fund their journalists appropriately. But back then I was on my own when it came to costs.

I paid for my own first 3G iPhone, a brick by today's standards. Looking back, I'm amazed it was able to publish a tweet fast enough to meet the expectations of live online coverage that was radically reshaping the way politics was being reported. But at the time it was a gateway to success. Of course, data costs were high and there was no such thing as office or public wifi at Parliament House, so any money I could have been using to pay off my credit card now went towards my astronomical phone bills instead.

And so I had entered myself in the awards for the coverage I'd done, partly on social media, of the 2009 leadership spill in which Malcolm Turnbull was replaced by Tony Abbott (who would, two elections later, become prime minister). Of course I hoped that I would win, not least because I had spent so much of my own money on phone bills, but I didn't expect to, because I was up against some seriously good yarns by impressive journos.

As they began announcing the category winners, my phone started buzzing. I left the function to pick up my voicemail. The ABC's Mark Simkin and Chris Uhlmann were reporting that Kevin Rudd was about to be rolled as prime minister. My news editor was asking what I knew and could I file something on it.

What? This must be a joke, I thought. This couldn't possibly be happening. I texted the media guys in the Prime Minister's Office and a few Labor MPs. The MPs I was able to contact knew nothing, but the answer from the Prime Minister's Office was vague: enough to confirm something was up. Could Kevin Rudd, the people's prime minister, elected just over two years ago in a wave of feel-good sentiment, really be on the verge of being dumped by his own party?

While I was firing off texts and taking and making calls to contacts, the MC announced my name as the winner for the radio division, which meant I was in the running for the top award. By the time I was named the overall winner, it was established that the push was on to roll Kevin Rudd. I barely remember my speech, but I do recall saying something like, 'I'm accepting this award for my coverage of a leadership spill, but there's another one taking place in Canberra right now.' Later someone told me that the room virtually emptied when I said those words.

I was thrilled to win the award but there was literally no time to celebrate. I had flown to Sydney but needed to be back in Canberra before dawn, which meant driving. I detoured via St Leonards, picked up one of the news cars and was on the road back to Canberra by midnight so I could man 'the doors' of Parliament and quiz Labor MPs as they arrived for work as to what Kevin Rudd's fate would be. The rest, as they say, is history: Rudd was out, to be replaced by Australia's first female prime minister, Julia Gillard.

The week was a mixture of excitement, adrenaline and sadness. I barely had time to register what winning the award meant—a trip to London and my first opportunity to visit the United States and finally cut up that credit card. But the ugliness of what had taken place in Canberra was all too visible, not just on Kevin Rudd's face as he blubbed during his final press conference, but also on his staff, many of whom had become friends we journalists dealt with daily, who were also suddenly out of a job. It may have been the come-down from the adrenaline or the red wine that I'd reflect over at the end of each leadership spill I have covered, but they always left me a little sadder than before and dispirited about just how brutal politics can be when raw power is at stake.

It wasn't just my professional life that was blossoming. In 2010 I met my partner Graham, an economist who had wooed me online by tweeting to me about standard deviation and why I should look for the long-term trends in the unemployment rate and disregard the incremental movements in the monthly statistics. Sexy stuff!

I'm not the type to spend my days wistfully longing to be proposed to and dreaming of rushing down the aisle in a mess of white tulle. But after one boyfriend, four years of singledom, two failed attempts at relationships and too many hopeless dates to want to remember, I knew when we first met in real life (more than a year after we started tweeting to each other about the efficacy of the Rudd government's economic stimulus program) that Graham was *the one*.

Then in December I got a new job as a political reporter with the ABC, moving from my two-person 2UE press gallery bureau to an office down the corridor bursting with thirty or so journalists, plus camera operators, editors and studio crew. They had a combined experience of several hundred years and I was keen to learn all I could about covering politics and breaking news from these wise heads. There was so much going on that India had to sit at the back of my mind while my life changed around me. Now wasn't the time to rock the boat or take my mind off work, I told myself.

In my most honest moments I admitted that one of the things I feared was having my perceptions of myself and my life smashed beyond repair by what I might see in India. I didn't want to have to feel guilty for enjoying the success that my career might bring. I didn't want to have to feel guilty for buying shoes or nice wine or whatever other indulgences I felt I had earned after years of living on a shoestring budget. I didn't want to have to think about the fact that I was enjoying things that came at a price that could save lives somewhere far away, lives of people just like I might have been.

I secretly feared that the sight of their poverty would force me to justify myself twice over—once in the way that any Australian with enough money to travel would have to when confronted by the sights of the developing world, but doubly so, because unlike most Australians, I had been lifted out of there by the hand of fate. I was afraid that once I saw the misery I had escaped, I would (somehow) be shamed into changing my life.

As well as what it might do to me psychologically, I also feared the physical reality of such a trip. The only travelling I had done in Asia really didn't count—a quick stop in Singapore and a recent beach holiday at a Four Seasons resort in Langkawi, Malaysia. Was I ready for unvarnished truth? I had spent so many years dwelling on the horrors of India that I couldn't imagine any positives. How could you enjoy a beautiful sight in the background if the foreground was filled with scores of maimed beggars? Everything you ate and drank could make you horribly sick. Every mosquito carried malaria and dengue fever. There would be filth everywhere. And yet . . . I couldn't let go of the idea.

My curiosity about the world was what drove me to become a journalist. I love learning. Seeking information is what I love to do from the moment I wake up, when I roll over and grab my phone to check the news feed, to the moment I set my phone on charge and place it under my pillow before I go to sleep. So it was an unpleasant realisation to have to admit that my prejudices about India had shut down my natural curiosity. I'd developed a blind spot, despite my long-held beliefs that prejudice is fed by fear and that fear is the most corrosive and disabling instinct of all.

In fact, my wilful ignorance went so deep that it was only after seeing *Slumdog* that I learned, to my mortification, that I didn't even have the details of where I came from right. I was born in the city of Bettiah in the state of Bihar. But somewhere along the line I had got the idea that they were one and the same place, a city that was spelled Bettiah but pronounced Bihar. If people asked where in India I was from I would say, 'Bihar, spelled *Bettiah*.' Occasionally Indian taxi drivers would press me to say it again, but they never corrected me. Perhaps my abrasiveness at the initial question deterred them from telling me that mistaking Bettiah for Bihar was the equivalent of confusing Bathurst for New South Wales. When I finally did google 'Bettiah', post-*Slumdog*, and saw the mistake I'd been making all those years, I flushed hot with shame.

Despite all the reasons I gave myself for not going, the idea of visiting India persisted. I raised the idea with Graham. He was instantly excited at the thought of it and hugely supportive of my wish to risk going off the beaten track to see the place where I'd been born. His support and enthusiasm was the difference between maybe and definitely. I doubted I could do it alone, logistically or, more importantly, emotionally. If I fell apart, I wanted someone there to catch me.

So in mid-2011 we set a date for our trip: January 2012. This would be summer holiday time in Australia, making it easier for us to get time off, and the cool season in India. We would go for nine days, starting with four days in Delhi, then on to Bihar for two nights and then back to Delhi, with an obligatory day trip to Agra to see the Taj Mahal.

But having decided to go did not mean my fears disappeared. The way I dealt with them was by not dealing with anything. I developed the most bizarre avoidance of all the details I'd usually attend to well before a trip. Normally I would prepare months ahead, writing up lists of what to pack, poring over TripAdvisor's 'Things to Do' recommendations, drawing up lists of where we'd eat, tour and stay then obsessively entering it all into my computer calendar, complete with corresponding time zones. But the weeks ticked by and I did nothing except book a hotel in Delhi. I didn't buy guidebooks, I didn't study online ratings, I didn't hunt down great restaurants. It was Graham who later bought the guidebooks and warned me to check whether I'd need a special visa as a journalist, as is the case in many countries.

It was only in December 2011, a month before we were due to go, that I began seriously preparing. Only then did I check on the medical recommendations and legal requirements, loosely work up a plan for the problem of how to get to Bihar—something Graham ended up solving through one of

his Indian-born colleagues. The normal excitement of travelling was there, but this time it was completely overwhelmed
by worry and fear. Usually I tackled problems through hard
work, persistence or just choosing not to worry about them.
I couldn't do any of that in this instance. I couldn't choose
not to worry about very real fears that were gnawing at my
stomach every time I even began to think about how the trip
might go.

Finally, just weeks before our 8 January departure date,
I set about sorting out vaccinations. Blessed with good health,
I rarely visit the doctor, but I made an appointment at a local
GP surgery that was able to fit me in straight away. As it
turned out, my doctor was originally from India. She was the
first Indian person I'd actually had a conversation with since
the flights had been booked.

In order to determine what shots I would need, she asked
where in India I was going. When I answered, her reaction
shocked me. 'Bihar, why would you go there?' she said sharply.
'What, are you from there?' Haltingly, I said yes. All I really
knew about Bihar was what I had gleaned when I googled
'Bettiah' that lone time. I vaguely knew its geographic location
within India, up in the north-east, bordering Nepal. I knew
it was very poor. That was about it.

My doctor didn't know Bettiah but she knew Bihar well.
She had spent some time working there, and her impressions
of the state were far from kind. 'It's backward, discriminatory,

corrupt and most of all dangerous,' she said harshly. 'Any time you are asked for a bribe, just pay it.'

I already knew Bihar would be the hardest part of the trip, and not just the emotional aspect of returning to the orphanage where I had spent my first few months. It would also be the most challenging section logistically. As I later learned for myself, India's capital, Delhi, is easy to navigate from afar; it deals with tourists all the time, it's a major city. But when I finally put my mind to organising the Bihar leg of the trip, I was stunned to learn that there wasn't even a hotel where we could stay.

Later that night, with fear gnawing at me, I watched a YouTube video clip of Bettiah. It was clearly taken from a camera strapped to a pushbike being ridden around the city. City? Scrap that. I wouldn't call this a city, or even a town. A hovel. A dump. A dive. Like much of India, I would learn, there was dirt where the roads and footpaths should have been. The buildings looked like they wanted to lie down and die. This was real poverty. Panic rushed through me and I wanted to call the whole thing off and stay in Canberra for the summer. 'I'm not ready for this,' I told myself.

Pride beat my fear. But only just. I had told my family, made plans with Graham and begun to tell a few close friends about the trip. I didn't want to squib it in their eyes, or my own. I kept most of the worries to myself. Anyway, how could anyone else understand? Wouldn't they think I was being silly? Emotional? Vacuous, even? After all, why should I be so much more frightened than anyone else to see poverty? I did tell Mum about the video, though. She hadn't been to Bihar, and I described what I had seen. 'It doesn't even look like a real city,' I told her, feeling turmoil in my stomach. Mum could sympathise. While she didn't know Bihar she'd seen enough of India to imagine. But she recounted her memories, warmly, and I reminded myself of the millions of tourists who had gone before me.

My glimpse of the reality of what I was facing further paralysed me, and it was almost Christmas when I finally applied for a visa to enter the country. I started filling out the form online. Like all foreign visa applications it was a laborious process, and I seemed to have been working on it for hours when I arrived at the 'Occupation' section right near the end. I had to choose from a drop-down menu. I've thought before when filling in travel forms that require my job title how nice it would be to lie and say I pack cans in a factory. That way I could travel under the radar in a way that being marked as a journalist prevents—even though my job has had nothing to do with any of the trips I've taken. But of course it's never worth the risk: a single Google search would reveal the truth. Sighing, I selected 'journalist'. Up popped a message telling me that I had to fill in a completely different type of application, regardless of whether or not I was doing any actual journalism in India. Gah!

So, new forms filled in, passport and verified photos in hand, I headed to the Indian consulate in Canberra's version of a CBD. Everything was going fine until we got to the country of birth. 'Have you relinquished your Indian citizenship?' the consulate officer asked me.

Huh? 'Well, no, but I'm an Australian, obviously,' I replied, gesturing at my Australian passport.

'But because you were once an Indian citizen you need to formally relinquish your citizenship,' she informed me.

'But I became an Australian citizen when I was nine and there's no dual citizenship arrangement between India and Australia. So I've already relinquished it, haven't I?' I could hear the pitch of my voice rising.

The woman serving me was very sorry, she said, but she needed to see my birth certificate and Australian citizenship certificate. The trouble was, I had no idea where either of these might be. I couldn't recall ever having seen the former, and I hadn't seen the latter since we left the mayor's office on the day I got it.

I spent a whole day in my garage, sweating and turning out boxes filled with ancient school diaries, shoeboxes of negatives, photo prints of England, and even an old perfume I'd worn on our family stay in England when I was fourteen that, when I smelled it, instantly revived memories of all those wonderful months. This memorabilia had survived moves between two flats in Bathurst, two in Sydney and three in Canberra and I only ever looked at it on occasions like this when I needed to extract some sort of documentation to prove who I was. My efforts ended without me finding either of the documents I needed. It turned out that English-born Mum was naturalised at the same time as Damian and me, so our 'citizenship certificates' were nothing more than a formal note of our names on the back of hers.

Christmas was fast approaching and the number of working days available to process a visa was rapidly diminishing. Consular officials then informed me that the other approach I could take was to have my original Indian passport, on which I had travelled to Australia as a baby, invalidated by the Indian High Commission, also in Canberra. To do this I would have to provide a statutory declaration verifying that I am indeed an Australian citizen.

Fortunately, turning up my Indian passport proved easier than finding the other material. The first time I had seen it was when it surfaced in my bedroom one day when I was a teenager. I don't know how it got there—I suppose Mum came across it and thought I might like it. It was a little black-covered booklet complete with an unrecognisable photo of chubby-cheeked baby me. Back then I had shrugged and tossed it in a bottom drawer with all the other junk I never looked at. When I packed up my bedroom at seventeen to leave for my year in

England, the passport joined old cassettes, debating speeches written out on palm cards, sports carnival ribbons, and letters from high school crushes which were occasionally reciprocated, all packed away in shoeboxes that I stored in the shed.

Somehow it had survived my various moves since then. At one point I'd come close to throwing it out, thinking there was no point in keeping it. I tossed it into a garbage bag, then extracted it at the last minute, out of some dutiful sense that I should preserve my history, if only for Mum's sake. All those years later, I gave thanks for that twinge of conscience as I frantically zipped between the nearest available justice of the peace and the two Indian diplomatic agencies (each located on opposite sides of the lake, of course).

On payment of a fee, the High Commission formally revoked the passport, allowing the visa office to process my application. As this was being done I laughingly told the women behind the counter how farcical this had all been for me—that I was not Indian and never had been, and that relinquishing something I didn't even know I had was absurd. 'But you are Indian,' said one of the ladies, puzzled. Out of politeness I didn't reply, but I thought loud and clear, 'Oh no, I'm not!'

A few days later I got a call from the High Commission: they were examining my paperwork and called because they needed proof of my citizenship. My heart sank. Mother of God, not this again. I tried not to sound hysterical as

I explained the process I'd gone through. Eventually the gentleman was convinced that the application could proceed, though he warned me that journalist visas could take a month to process.

To my huge relief I got a call two days before my departure telling me that my visa was ready for collection. I was all smiles walking in to collect it, until one of the women helping me said, 'You know there's a visa for former citizens you can get? It's just as good as having dual citizenship and then you wouldn't have to worry about going through the extra journalist visa application.' I gaped at her, willing my head not to collapse into my hands. 'Yes,' she continued kindly, 'you can get it for your next trip.' I made a polite noise, trying not to look sceptical. 'There won't be a next trip,' I thought.

Over the Christmas period I went to my parents' place for a few days. Not long after I arrived, Mum got out the orange manila folder in which she had kept all my adoption papers and other documents over the years, and we went through them together. They had always been available to me, but this was the first time I had been interested enough to look at them properly. Mum was excited for me about the trip. She smiled wistfully as she remembered back to 1984. We sat on the lounge together and she examined each piece of correspondence and explained them to me. We read over each letter, Mum pausing now and then as the precious typed blue aerogrammes sparked another memory to share. I took note of the addresses of the two orphanages where I had been cared for, one in Fakirana in Bihar and the other in Delhi, and in the following days sent off letters explaining who I was and asking if I might be permitted to visit. I noted my full contact details, including my email address.

I didn't hear back from Holy Cross in Delhi (I would just have to call them when I arrived), but within days I received an affectionate email from a Sister Lissil in Bihar. Although it was no longer an orphanage, having become a kind of multi-purpose education centre and home for the destitute, she assured me that Graham and I would be very welcome, and finished by conveying 'love from all the Sisters at your home in Fakirana'. The warmth in every word was a huge relief.

Among my presents that Christmas was a book from Dad that became the first of many, many books about India I would go on to collect. It was *Behind the Beautiful Forevers* by Katherine Boo, and it's still one of the best portrayals of the country I have read. Boo is a journalist who was living in India when she decided to document the lives of the residents of a slum on the other side of a huge 'Beautiful Forever' sign from Mumbai airport. Her depiction of the hopelessness that pervades so many of the people's lives, the complexities of the drudgery of poverty, the substance abuse, the slum politics between the families, the toll it takes on mental health, is unforgettable. But as brilliant as the book was, it didn't exactly reassure me about what I was about to experience. In any event, could I have done any amount of research that would have prepared me for this highly personal journey? I doubted it.

6

MY FIRST TASTE OF INDIA

Before leaving, I had wondered whether I was duty bound to try to replicate how I might have lived had I not been adopted. Wasn't that the *real* India I should get to know? But Mum quickly put a stop to that way of thinking. There was no point risking my health or safety, she said. So we didn't skimp. We booked the best and most central hotel in Delhi as recommended by TripAdvisor, the Imperial.

As with landing in any country for the first time, my immediate impression was of the airport. It left Sydney's poor old Kingsford Smith for dead—huge, clean, modern and dramatically decorated. Customs, baggage collection and immigration were all an orderly breeze. Given my diet of foreign news, I'd been expecting to be wowed by India's booming modernisation, and this first glimpse didn't disappoint.

One of the advantages in splashing out on the Imperial was that hotel transfers were included. I didn't want to have to be worrying about touts when I arrived, jetlagged and in who knew what kind of emotional state. I'm almost ashamed to admit it, it's so clichéd, but within minutes the hotel driver and I were exchanging cricketer stories. I whipped out my phone to show a photo of myself with my favourite cricketer, Michael Bevan. But I was outdone, because the Australian cricket team had stayed at the Imperial. The driver's favourites were Ricky Ponting and Glenn McGrath, and he had pictures of himself with both of them to show off to me.

Dad, Rani and Damian love sport. It seemed to be always on TV in the background when we were in high school, much to Mum's disgust, and mine. They'd watch it all, rugby league, golf, the tennis and the cricket. It didn't matter if it was summer or winter, there seemed to be no reprieve from sport on the box. Golf makes me sleepy and I wince at tackles in rugby league or union, but in my high school years I did begin to enjoy a game of cricket or tennis.

One of the few games we all watched together as a family and with visiting friends was the 1996 one-dayer against the West Indies when Michael Bevan needed a four off the last ball to win the game. He smashed it to the boundary. It was a great night and made Bevan my high school crush for several years. More than ten years later I'd been sent to cover Kevin Rudd's announcement of the Prime Minister's XI at Manuka Oval in Canberra when who should pop up but Bevan-Heaven himself. I rarely ask anyone I meet in my professional capacity for a photo. Never a prime minister or a politician, but this was different. I roped my flatmate, Fairfax snapper Glen McCurtayne, into taking a quick shot. And now here I was in India using one of the most hackneyed Indian–Australian icebreakers—cricket! The conversation flowed easily, and in no time we were in the gleaming black four-wheel drive and off through night-time Delhi, bound for the hotel.

Orange streetlights loomed out of the mist and disappeared again. In 2012 the city was home to nearly 17 million (almost another million more now) and I'd expected everywhere I looked to be teeming with people, so it was eerie to be driving along what appeared to be nearly empty streets.

Arriving at the hotel was my first introduction to the two Indias I would come to know, and despair of. It was the first country I'd been to where we were screened through metal detectors and our hand luggage x-rayed before we entered the hotel door. Given that the Mumbai attacks—in which terrorists attacked several sites in south Mumbai, including two five star hotels, killing 164 people in a series of bombings and shootings over four days—had taken place three years earlier, I was reassured, but it was jolting nevertheless. Such innocence we enjoy in Australia, even though we are of course never immune.

Once inside, the Imperial is unadulterated Raj-era opulence. The foyer is tiled with great slabs of polished white marble. A well-lit Chanel boutique jumps immediately into your eyeline. We weren't hungry, just sleepy, so we checked in and went straight to our room. The hallway connecting the foyer to the lifts and rooms was lined with elephant statues, exquisite sculptures and paintings. I've been fortunate enough to have stayed at some very luxurious hotels around the world but none of them are as sumptuous and lavish as India's. Perhaps it's knowing that they sit amid so much need that makes the impression particularly sharp.

After a few hours' sleep we woke to see the sun starting to break through the fog, though there was no warmth in its winter rays. Breakfast and tea 'was taken', as the Indians say. I had vowed to eat nothing but Indian food from the moment we arrived to the day we left, and I instantly loved it. We made a glorious start to the day with plates piled high with *parathas* (stuffed flatbreads), *vadas* (lentil fritters), *dosas* (lentil crepes), *upma* (savoury semolina porridge) and *idlis* (steamed rice cakes), all topped with coconut chutneys and searing chilli powders.

Something strange had happened to me over the previous two years or so. Food in Australia was never hot enough for me—I mean chilli hot, not heated. I'd always liked a little spice, but by the time I hit my late twenties I couldn't get enough heat in my food. The only thing that ever really satisfied me was huge lumps of wasabi on my sashimi. I'd load up enough to make my nose burn and my eyes water. The food at the Imperial was made for western palettes and milder than normal, but it was still spicier than what I ate at home. I had never properly tried Indian cuisine in Australia, and now it delighted my tastebuds.

Finally I was ready to take my first steps outside the hotel, an enclave of luxury whose gorgeous grounds are walled off from the real India beyond. This was it. There was no going back. My feelings were a whirl of hope and dread.

We decided to begin our travels in the same way we would in any other city—by exploring on foot. We walked with no specific direction or purpose other than to see, absorb and slowly breathe in the city. Knowing that Indian dress standards were traditionally modest, I had come prepared, covered neck to toe with loose-fitting clothes, and underneath them was a money belt strapped around my waist with all my cards and cash safely tucked away. I was ready for the haggling that would take place any time we wanted to buy something. I had decided that I wouldn't bargain too hard—I was determined not to be *that* kind of western visitor, plundering Asia for bargains. But I didn't anticipate the touts, the sheer number of them and their persistent refusal to take 'no' for an answer. They were everywhere! Sensing our lack of purpose, they lined our path asking whether we'd like a car, a tuk-tuk, a guide. Heck, they would have carried us if we'd let them. Our polite but—we thought—firm refusals only seemed to make them more insistent.

It only took about thirty minutes until we were worn into submission. The lucky tuk-tuk driver to whom we finally said yes told us his name was Bobby. He was a thin, impeccably dressed young man with a wide smile and moustache to match. He talked even faster than he drove, telling us about how he was trying to earn enough to get an education for his wife and his child and overflowing with ideas about what we should do on our first day.

It was my first ride in a tuk-tuk (a covered, three-wheeled auto rickshaw), and I'm grateful now that I hadn't come across India's road statistics at the time. In 2012, when we visited, the government recorded just under half a million road accidents, resulting in more than 142,000 deaths. India's roads don't just look chaotic, they're genuinely dangerous. No wonder climbing into Bobby's tuk-tuk reminded me of getting on a theme park adventure ride.

Tuk-tuks are wild fun. There are no seatbelts, of course. Only a piece of black leather, the 'hood' around the passengers, separates you from the mayhem. You don't even have to fully extend your arm to touch the cars, motorbikes and fellow tuk-tuks surrounding you in Delhi's endless traffic jams. The congestion means the traffic moves excruciatingly slowly, except for those moments when you hurtle forward into a sudden opening.

We settled on Delhi's green hub, the beautiful Lodi Gardens, as our destination. Graham and I had thought Bobby would simply drop us off there. No dice. Instead, he insisted on accompanying us. The Gardens are huge: a free-to-enter slice of peace in the crowded, hectic capital and host to the towering tombs of India's medieval rulers Muhammad Shah and Sikander Lodi. There are few plaques to inform you about what you're seeing; as I would learn later, the custom is to hire a trained guide. That would have been handy, but instead we had ever-smiling Bobby providing not entirely convincing explanations of the Gardens' features. To be honest, I would rather have consulted Wikipedia, but Bobby wouldn't leave no matter how many times we protested that we were finished for the day, thanked him and attempted to say goodbye.

At lunchtime we made for the entrance to the upmarket Lodi Garden Restaurant. I could sense that Graham's relief matched mine as we paid Bobby for his services. In fact, we overpaid him. We knew we were doing so, but it was part politeness, part guilt, and mostly intended to signal that our time together was over.

We should have thought that one through. If we had, we would have realised that after such largesse Bobby would be crazy to let us out of his sight. He repeatedly promised to wait outside the gate for us to finish so he could take us shopping (in my earlier nervous excitement I had babbled on about wanting to shop up a storm, with placemats, cushion covers, statues and maybe some jewellery all on my wish list). As we disappeared into the restaurant we kept assuring him that we were fine, thanks, and besides we'd be a very long time at lunch.

It was odd. I kept expecting to *feel* something on that first day. I'm here, in India, I kept telling myself. But no emotion came. I was happy to be in Delhi, that was something. I certainly didn't hate it, and I was finding myself surprisingly open to everything I saw and curious about every difference between my two countries. But it felt odd to be sitting and eating in the country that had served for so long as my mental bogeyman and not feeling the emotions I had expected to feel.

When we'd finished our leisurely meal, we talked about what to do if Bobby was still waiting for us. Like criminals, we poked our heads around the corner of the restaurant's wall to scout out the situation. We looked for him in the long line of tuk-tuk drivers but couldn't spot him. Relieved, but not taking any chances of getting hooked by another driver, we scurried out as quickly and discreetly as we could. After walking rapidly for about a kilometre we finally slowed down and began to relax.

We'd walked for about the same distance again, enjoying the sights and sounds, when a tuk-tuk puttered past, then came to a sudden stop ahead of us. As we watched, an elderly

Indian lady carrying shopping bags was evicted from it onto the footpath and a wiry figure emerged from the driver's seat. Bobby.

Delighted to have found us again, he wouldn't take no for an answer to his suggestion that he take us to 'Art India', a store he'd been extolling all morning as containing India's 'finest quality'. I was still then naive enough not to realise that everyone trying to sell something to a foreigner in India offers only 'finest quality'. From faux marble figurines to cheap cushion covers, it was all 'finest quality'. If nothing else, we had to admire Bobby's tenacity as we set off for the store, which he promised was 'just down this road'.

Fifteen minutes later, the tuk-tuk rattled to a stop. The knowing nod exchanged by Bobby and the shop's owner said it all. It's the oldest trick in the book, literally: all the guidebooks warn that drivers are paid commissions to deliver tourists to stores. Us being brought here had nothing to do with quality items; it was a business transaction. Everyone inside was a tourist and, as I would later confirm, the prices were at least 20 per cent above what they'd be in street markets and emporiums. I felt obliged to buy a few things, but afterwards Graham and I said firmly that we wanted to be taken back to the hotel. Non-negotiable. Bobby heard the determination in our voices and for once didn't demur.

When he finally dropped us at the Imperial as darkness fell, I was beat. The constant negotiating just to be left alone while trying to stay polite and patient was exhausting. If India was going to be a constant battle like this, I didn't know how I'd last. 'Welcome back home,' the Imperial staff greet visitors as they walk through the door. It had seemed a bit over the top to me that morning, but right now I felt nothing but relief and gratitude for this impeccable sanctuary.

Each day brought challenges and delights. One morning strolling a crowded tourist market off Delhi's Connaught Place I fell victim to another of the tricks the guidebooks had warned about. 'Madame, Madame, there's shit on your shoe,' a young man walking quickly alongside me said. I suspected something was up and tried to ignore him—politely, of course. Until Graham whispered to me 'I hate to say it but you actually do have shit on your shoe.' Sure enough I looked down to find a glistening glob of crap on my right foot. I refused to let them clean it knowing that was the moment they'd try to deprive my pockets of any cash I might have been silly enough to leave there. (I hadn't of course). No, I'd do it myself. I cursed the whole episode but at the same time said to Graham 'if this is the worst thing that happens to us while we're in India it's going to be a great trip.' It was. We were as careful as we could be and never felt in any danger. Occasionally we'd feel our pockets being thoroughly scoped out by some sticky fingers but we never filled them with anything worth taking. That night, having dinner in the hotel restaurant, Graham nudged me. 'That's Yoko Ono,' he said. Sure enough, it was. We couldn't resist eavesdropping on her elaborate order for special fruits and juices. Amazing, I thought, one minute you're cleaning the crap off your shoe that someone threw on you in the hope of making a few rupees, and the next you can be sitting next to Yoko Ono. India was a land of contrasts, all right.

We spent a few days in Delhi doing touristy things. We tried out the brilliantly clean, newly constructed Metro; haggled with the spirited ladies at Janpath market for beautiful shawls and brightly coloured cushion cases; and looked longingly at the street food stalls, wondering if we could risk shocking our tummies with the local fare but deciding against it for the moment.

And then we had one of the most profound experiences of our lives. We went on a walking tour of Old Delhi designed to show visitors to India the reality of life for children living on the street. The true heart of the capital, Old Delhi was once a Mughal capital and unlike New Delhi, is extremely dilapidated and crowded with marketplaces, mosques and medieval walls and gates. The tour was run by a charitable organisation called the Salaam Baalak Trust, founded by popular Indian film director Mira Nair and named for her 1988 film *Salaam Bombay!* The film is an incredibly sad story about street kids in Bombay (Mumbai), including a young girl forced into prostitution and the boy (anti)hero who tries and fails to save her. In some ways, *Salaam Bombay!* feels like a precursor to *Slumdog Millionaire*. The plot is fictional but most of the young cast really were street children when they were given the roles. *Salaam* is just as compelling as *Slumdog* but far more gritty and understated; many in India regard it as a more authentic version of the experience of such children.

Mira Nair used the proceeds of the film to establish the Salaam Baalak Trust, which devotes itself to helping India's street children in cities such as Mumbai and Delhi. As well as the direct, practical help of providing children with homes, and education and training for older orphans, another of its aims is to show people the realities of these children's lives. It does this through these two-hour guided group walks. The guides are all former street children who have been helped out of that life by the Trust, and the Delhi tours begin in the giant central railway station, a place which has become 'home' to many of these children.

This tour was a gem I'd found on TripAdvisor. At the airport in Sydney before we boarded I'd belatedly begun to look up the sights we really couldn't return home without seeing. But I was on the lookout for 'real' experiences. I was conscious that staying in such a ritzy hotel we'd be cloistered from the India that I needed to see, felt obliged to see and wanted to see. This wasn't just a holiday, after all. A quick email once we were in Delhi was all it took to book in for the street walk the next day.

Our guide was a beautiful, shyly confident young man named Satyender. He was not yet twenty but he spoke and carried himself with the assurance of an older man. He told us he had become a street child after fleeing his violent father in the north of India. Like the other children with no homes and no other way to provide for themselves, he had been forced to do whatever it took to survive. He calmly described how children like him fall prey to gangs, forced to steal, beg and cheat to serve their gang lords or the addictions they are led into. He spoke in a matter-of-fact manner that suggested he had long since made peace with all that had happened to him. I was moved to tears by his story but was embarrassed to cry when he showed no pain himself. I tried unsuccessfully to blink away my tears, and I wasn't the only one to weep. Until that moment I don't think I'd ever fully appreciated the gift of innocence among so many other wonderful aspects of my safe, happy Australian childhood.

There were just over a dozen of us in the tour group, all foreigners, from countries including Germany and Britain, with some other Australians, and ranging in age from gap-year backpackers to couples in their forties and fifties. As different as we were from one another, we were all on one side of a chasm of experience and Satyender was on the other. He had a different kind of maturity. He was so young yet he could hold the absolute attention of this disparate group. He was a beautiful man in so many ways, not least his gentle patience with our personal questions, including whether he'd ever seen his family again (no), and how he felt about it (at peace).

The tour wound through Old Delhi. Rubbish was heaped wherever seemed convenient. Feral dogs slept anywhere and everywhere. Visually everything looked like one giant mess. Electrical wires hung low and in bunches. Advertising signs would be tacked on to any vertical surface but it didn't matter if they hung straight or not. There was little sense of privacy. It was nothing to walk by someone's house and see a partially clothed man washing himself. Children in Tommy Hilfiger tops ran around playing and looking shyly at us foreigners. The violence, abuse, neglect and fractured families that were woven into the lives of the street children stemmed from one core problem: poverty. I'd expected to see this poverty in the form of beggars, but they were surprisingly few and far between. However, I knew from Boo's book that the poverty was also written in all the things I couldn't expect to see at first glance: the domestic abuse, suicides, alcoholism and drug addiction.

Satyender explained that the children would be sent out by the gang leaders to carry out dubious sorts of work. One such job was collecting detritus to sell. He introduced us to the adult rubbish collectors/recyclers, sitting in front of a heap of litter with their rusting set of scales. We watched as they paid the street children a few rupees for the most recyclable trash from their haul. (Now I understood the advice to tourists to crush plastic water bottles before throwing them out, lest they be retrieved, refilled with contaminated water and sold to an unsuspecting visitor).

We poked our heads into a dingy room that housed two ancient gaming machines. They were so old that I wondered whether they could even crank to life, but we learned that they were potent lures and potential addictions for street children. Who wouldn't want a few minutes of electronic relief from what could only be a hellish way of living? What happened to the ones Salaam Baalak couldn't reach, couldn't save?

The tour ended on a happy note at the Trust's crammed shelters, where we met a roomful of young boys, colouring in and quietly chatting with each other. A French volunteer was looking after them. She spoke to us briefly, urging us to send paper, crayons and pencils if we wanted to contribute.

Finally the tour was over and it was time for us to pay. The cost was two hundred rupees each—about four Australian dollars. I nearly wept again. In this India, I found constantly, people had so little and asked for so little when they should have wanted so much more. We quadrupled the amount and still felt guilty that it was, to us, almost nothing—the cost of no more than six coffees back at Aussies Cafe in Parliament House. A couple of days' worth of caffeine.

Our next experience was more personal, a visit to the Delhi orphanage where I'd stayed after being moved from Bihar and before I was sent to Sydney. It was now called the Holy Cross Social Service Centre. They hadn't replied to my letter, and since arriving in Delhi I'd tried calling the phone number on the old letters but it didn't work. Mum's advice had been just to turn up. On the afternoon of our third day in Delhi, we got into a cab at the Imperial's taxi stand for a journey back to a place of which I had no memory but which had been a crucial staging post in my own passage from India.

Our driver's name was Titoo, and his car was immaculate. It didn't stay that way for long. Delhi is a sprawling city and the orphanage is on its outskirts. We drove for forty minutes along roads that got narrower and narrower until they were little more than dusty, pothole-riddled laneways. Sitting in the back, Graham and I were largely silent. It was our first long drive through Delhi's outer suburbs and we were absorbed in the sights. My silence also concealed my nerves. If I'd been a fingernail biter I would have had no nails left. I tried to distract myself with the sights around me, discreetly taking photos on my phone whenever I could, of what Indians probably think are just regular-looking streets but which to me were complex visual puzzles, with wiring hanging here, traffic dodging there and dilapidated houses lining them all.

As we edged closer to the fringes of Delhi, the light began to retreat from the day. It became obvious that Titoo didn't know exactly where to go, and I became more stressed and anxious, worried we might not make it there before night-time.

By contrast, Titoo himself was a model of serenity. Indian taxi drivers are professionals who take great pride in getting you safely to your destination, however slow or tedious the route. Titoo was no exception. Even though he had to stop three times to ask for directions, he showed no concern—not a bead of sweat or even a frown—as we went deep into some of Delhi's poorest suburbs, with the dusk gathering around us.

Several thousand rupees later, we pulled up in front of a gated property resembling a terraced string of houses on one of the nicer streets of this neglected district. Titoo parked and settled in to wait as Graham and I walked up to investigate. My immediate impression was that the orphanage was unwelcoming. A gate stood high and there were no signs to distinguish it from any of the other private houses in the same row. It felt like we shouldn't be intruding. Discovering that the gate was unlocked, we cautiously entered the grounds and approached the building, which looked to be three or four storeys high. We could hear children's voices coming from the top floor. I knocked at the front door, but the ground floor was deserted and no one heard me.

It's never a comfortable experience venturing into a place where you're not expected. My heart was in my throat. If this went wrong, I thought, it would sour my whole 'India experience'. While Graham waited near the entrance, I climbed the stairs to the top floor, hoping they wouldn't mind my intrusion. It was very dark inside the building; the day's last rays of sun didn't penetrate far. Peering into the rooms off the stairway landing, I could make out children playing in what looked like a day care centre. Without even realising it, I was scanning all around trying to see if I could spot anything that matched the background of any of the photos taken of Damian and me during the months we had (separately) spent here.

I went into one of the rooms and approached some children aged three or four. They didn't speak much English but they ran off to find an adult, who in turn took me to one of the Holy Cross nuns. She seemed to know instantly who I was, and asked if I had written. 'Yes,' I nodded, smiling. She told me she had received my letter but that this was no longer the site of the orphanage. It had moved further out, but she was sure I would be warmly welcomed there. I was feeling immensely relieved when, armed with new directions, I went back down to tell Graham and Titoo.

The new site of the orphanage was ten minutes' drive away. On the way we passed a rubbish heap. High atop it was the most gorgeous little boy, maybe seven or eight, smiling as he skipped along. In one hand he held a white bucket painted with big bright pink flowers, and he was filling it with scraps he found rummaging through the garbage. There was no shame about it; he looked as content ferreting about in the rubbish heap as I remember feeling when I rummaged around the backyard at Hobbys for snails. Later I realised that this matter-of-fact acceptance of poverty is one of the things that both defines and curses India.

But when we arrived at the new Holy Cross Social Service Centre I could see straight away that it was one of the millions of Indian success stories. The new orphanage is a huge purpose-built brick complex circling an internal courtyard and is kept secure with a guard at the gate. I explained why we were there and he opened the gate and waved us through.

A nun greeted us with a warm smile and introduced herself as Sister Smigta. Aged maybe in her forties, she was one of those larger-than-life people: boisterous, generous, outgoing, friendly and kind. Of course I was welcome, she said, there was no question about it. This was my 'home', after all.

She introduced Graham and me to all the sisters, one a girl ten years younger than me who was in training to be a nun. The only nuns I'd known before were from Bathurst, always at the same Mass each week. They were similarly lovely but so *old*, in their seventies or eighties, wrinkled and frail. When I was in year twelve, our Studies of Religion teacher asked us each to write up on the whiteboard what we wanted to be when we grew up. I had no trouble: I already knew I wanted to be a journalist. Averil wrote lawyer. Rachal intended to be a physiotherapist. A few wrote up 'mother.' Our teacher remarked at how admirable it was that we as young women could choose our destiny, whether it be in the home or an office. No one wrote nun. Yet here was a teenager giving over her life to service. Each day in India, something would jolt me.

Sister Smigta took us into a cosy room with lounges and a television and sat us down with a cup of tea. Then she went and got the record book, which turned out to be the greatest welcome to India of all. A simple lined A4 book, it was filled with the names of all the children adopted through this orphanage, organised by date. Sister Smigta scanned through to find my entry and opened out the double page spread before me.

I was instantly drawn to the baby photos. There were two, one of which I'd seen before—a copy of it was in Mum's orange manila folder and another had been used for my Indian passport. It was a slightly dizzying moment, the first time I had seen something tangible in India to say that yes, I really had been here. I was filled with a tremendous joy. I couldn't stop smiling while at the same time my eyes filled with tears.

The hand-ruled columns contained my name, my birth date and birth place, the date when I came to Delhi, and my adoption details—Mum and Dad's address at the time, my adoption court case number and the date when I left Delhi for Australia. The entry contained fewer than a hundred words, but these brief sentences, numbers and dates combined to tell me the beginning of my story. I was looking at the evidence of my own life in a foreign land where the languages and customs were incomprehensible to me. It was an extraordinary, unique experience.

At Sister Smigta's request I filled in the blanks, the key details from the missing twenty-seven years, including entering my parents' current address and my own. Then she showed me Damian's pages, from two years before mine, and I updated his entry too.

Quite rightly I was not permitted to look at the pages belonging to other children who once lived at the orphanage—this is private information. But my mind was full of thoughts of all the lives contained in the pages of this unassuming ledger. They are adults now, like me, scattered around the world, separated by language and culture but linked by their common start in life. Adoption, already the most beautiful word in my vocabulary, grew even more exquisite and joyous to me.

After we had taken tea and cake, Sister Smigta showed us around the orphanage and introduced us to some of the children. They ranged from newborn babies still in their cots to children aged nine or ten. The first room was for the babies. They were so beautiful, all with huge eyes, just as we'd had in our baby photos. I could see how Mum would have fallen in love with her own new little babies as soon as she saw us. The second room in the corridor was for toddlers and for small children learning the alphabet and numbers. They were equally adorable.

We went downstairs to where a group of the older children aged eight and above were all playing. As soon as they saw us they formed several rows, as if in a choir and started singing. Their music was instantaneous and joyful. But I felt a pang in my heart for the toddlers and older kids. It was a terrific facility; the building was first class, with water, electricity, the works. The sisters caring for the children were tireless, with faces free from complaint. But still, these children were old enough that when they were eventually adopted out (as Sister Smigta said they all would be), they would remember the orphanage. I felt so very lucky that I was adopted so young and bonded with my parents before I was old enough to make memories.

Afterwards we met a well-dressed Indian gentleman who looked to be in his late thirties or early forties. He and his wife were unable to have children and were finalising their first adoption. Very few if any of the children here would be adopted out overseas like Damian, Rani and me. In fact, in 2013–14, just seven children from India were adopted to Australian parents, compared to thirty-three in 1988–89 (the earliest year the Australian Institute of Health and Welfare recorded country of origin for overseas adoptions). Nowadays, most are placed with Indian parents, largely due to legal changes around eligibility and a preference to keep orphaned children in their birth countries.

We'd brought a suitcase full of gifts for the orphanage and I asked Sister Smigta whether they would be of greater use in Delhi or in Bihar. There were no more children at Fakirana, she confirmed, and gladly took the suitcase, filled with toys by Mum and Melissa, off our hands. We left with our hearts in our mouths. There was so much to despair of in

India but also so much hope. While I wasn't naive enough to think that each adoption would go as smoothly and happily as mine, I felt uplifted after seeing the love bestowed on each and every child.

Titoo was waiting for us. The drive there had been an anxious and long one, but it felt like we arrived back at the gates of the Imperial in no time. I asked Titoo for his number—when we returned to Delhi, we'd get him to drive us again.

That night I went to bed full of emotion over what we had seen that day, and also with renewed nerves about the challenge we had to face tomorrow: getting to Bihar.

7

COMING 'HOME'

Bihar is the third most populous state in India, with nearly 9 per cent of the national population. Almost 55 per cent of its more than 100 million people live below the poverty line, and 36 million of them live in what the government defines as 'abject poverty'.

A few years ago, the World Bank pointed out that the poverty in Bihar was worse than in African countries including Malawi and Ghana. India's average literacy rate is just over 74 per cent, but in Bihar it is only 64 per cent. *The Economist* said that in addition to its many other problems, Bihar has been 'long blighted by caste politics'. Castes, determined at birth, govern a person's access to power depending on the status of their particular caste. There were many risks involved with travelling to Bihar. In 2012, police recorded nearly five thousand kidnappings in the state. Poor equals dangerous. But I didn't have a choice. I had to go there.

To get to Bettiah we first had to fly from Delhi to Bihar's capital, Patna. In order to enter an Indian airport you have to show your ID and valid ticket. The checkpoint at the Delhi domestic terminal was the first time during our trip that anyone tried to speak anything other than English to me. The security forces officer looked straight at me, not Graham, and began talking to me, presumably in Hindi. I looked at him, feeling almost guilty for not being able to understand him, but also surprised. I'd assumed, because I wore make-up and obviously western clothes (cargo pants, a slouchy jumper and a shawl over the top) and was travelling with white-man Graham, that they could easily tell I wasn't one of them, as such.

When I handed the security officer my Australian passport he flicked through it then looked up at me, straight in the eyes, smiled and said sorry in English. I was secretly a bit chuffed about his earlier assumption. In India, I didn't mind if someone thought I might understand Hindi. Instead I felt bad for not being able to respond. In the same way, I was finding I loved the food (why hadn't I believed Mum?). It was funny, the things I responded to here were all the things I had stupidly and immaturely run a million miles from when I was growing up. I could see the changes within myself and I liked them.

The flight to Patna was uneventful. We both already knew that what happened after we touched down would be the hardest part. What would Bihar and beyond bring us? Fortunately we weren't trying to do it all on our own. To my immense relief, Graham had a work associate whose cousin, Vikas, lived in Patna. Vikas greeted us at the airport wearing a t-shirt with a picture of the Sydney Harbour Bridge stretching across his chest and with an even wider smile on his face.

As we soon learned, many fewer people spoke English here than in Delhi and we really couldn't have arranged a car and driver on our own. Vikas had organised a driver called Ramesh for us, and in front of a big group of random onlookers and other drivers who were waiting for jobs, he made a show of punching his mobile number into Ramesh's Nokia and pressing a piece of paper into my hands with his contact details. Clearly the idea was that everyone in Patna would know about it if we went missing or if something else untoward happened to us. It was hugely reassuring, especially as Ramesh didn't speak English and we of course didn't know a word of Hindi.

Travelling around India had made me more aware of body language: when there's no other way of communicating, it signals so much. I was reassured by what I saw of Ramesh and the choices he made as soon as we got going. He was careful, attentive, patient and conscientious. Behind the wheel he was never in a hurry to overtake but nor did he loiter unnecessarily behind slower traffic. But even though I had a good feeling about him, we were in very risky territory, and it was comforting to know that we had the back-up of a mutual communication channel through Vikas if we needed it.

It took no time at all to realise that the plan Graham and I had initially discussed, of hiring a car and driving ourselves, would have been a total disaster. Thank goodness we'd been forced to abandon it when we discovered that visitors are not permitted to hire a car in India without also hiring a driver as a package deal. The reason we had considered it in the first place was that the distance from Patna to Bettiah is just 187 kilometres by road; in my ken that equated to roughly a three-hour drive. When I first moved to Canberra I regularly made the 300-kilometre drive back to Sydney without thinking twice. But this was another world.

Even before we left behind the relatively well-maintained roads of Patna it was clear to both of us that trying to drive ourselves would have induced an instant nervous breakdown. Just like everywhere else in India, the traffic was chaos, but here our driver also spent much of his time on the wrong side of the road, because the lane we should have been occupying was filled with all sorts of traffic all plodding along at different speeds: pedestrians, bicycles, tuk-tuks, hand-pulled rickshaws, buses, minivans and trucks covered with human cargo, not to mention the wandering cows for which all traffic must stop and wait.

Judging by the distance on the map, leaving Patna should have taken ten minutes. In reality it took nearly forty minutes. It felt as though we spent about half this time inching around one huge roundabout that seemed to exist not to facilitate traffic flow but to impede it, functioning as it did as a de facto marketplace, crammed with people, cows, horses and carts, so many goats and dogs and rickshaws, all the vehicles trapped, their impatient horns blowing louder and longer with every minute.

It's not just the traffic that makes driving in India an unthinkable task for tourists; in Bihar we couldn't pick up any 3G, something I hadn't even considered as a possibility. So much for relying on my iPhone's map. And then there are the roads themselves. The main road was actually in very good condition and seemed to have been laid relatively recently (by how many children, I wondered later), but other, smaller roads didn't deserve the name. They were more like goat tracks, and as we travelled along them I held my breath, hoping the jutting rocks didn't pop the tyres.

Just after we crossed the main bridge out of Patna, Ramesh gave me my first real scare. He'd been weaving through the men who walk among the moving cars selling banana bunches just plucked from the banks of the river below when he pulled over and stopped the car. He said something I couldn't understand, gesticulated and left. 'Oh my God, we're about to be kidnapped. This is it. This is the end,' I thought, somewhat melodramatically. 'Everything I've feared about Bihar is about to come true!' I sank lower in the seat, expecting a gang of men to set upon us at any minute.

'Where's he gone?' I asked Graham, panicking.

Ever cool in a crisis, real or not, he just shrugged his shoulders. 'He's probably just going to the toilet.'

My jaw was clenched so hard I was grinding my teeth. But Graham's guess was right: Ramesh was merely relieving himself. I'd say 'going to the toilet', only there was no toilet. Looking back along the bank, I saw him only about a metre from a woman who was doing the same thing, squatting by the side of the road. I felt instantly ashamed that I had witnessed them and robbed them of their dignity, but maybe the shame was all mine. Life in India is raw and unfiltered.

Because of my failure to perform my customary research, I was also taken by surprise by how much of Bihar was rural. Before I'd watched the YouTube video, I'd imagined Bettiah, for instance, to be a dirty but functioning metropolis, with young girls who had been forced into prostitution (could my mother have been one?) pounding grey concrete pavements, below city skylines. The video had disabused me of those notions, but even so I wasn't prepared for the reality. In Bihar, an astonishing 89 per cent of the population is rural, and as soon as we left the city I began to understand what that means. In Old Delhi the roadside electricity wires looped down lower than Melbourne's tram wiring, but on the rural roads we were now travelling they were sometimes non-existent, sometimes sagging along until they reached a pole where the loose wires hung down, and sometimes crudely knotted to connect the various strands. No wonder the power was intermittent.

The quality of the housing worsened the further we got from Patna. There were some clean, well-maintained buildings, but they were the exception. Close to the city, the norm was multi-storey concrete or rough brick homes with glassless windows. Many of them had clothes of the brightest colours flapping from the window frames, against the exteriors of the buildings, which were nearly always filthy, stained with pollution and grime. It was odd to see beautiful clean clothes drying against the dirt. The further out we went, the more basic the housing became. In the countryside the huts were made of mud, straw and bamboo. Here the brilliantly coloured saris hung on bamboo clotheslines where cows and goats congregated, with rubbish mounds nearby. Women and men slept on mounds of hay out the front of their huts, next to the animals. I guessed the insides of the huts to be mud. It was winter, so night fell early and the fog hung around until the middle of the day. Yet this was the most pleasant season: I realised just how brutal the summer and monsoon weather must be.

With a sudden rush I understood that if I had stayed here, my life wouldn't be the *Slumdog Millionaire* or *Salaam Bombay!* street-kid existence; it would most likely have been the almost medieval grind of this rural poverty. People throughout Bihar talked about how things had improved in the state over the past decade, particularly since Nitish Kumar became the state's chief minister in 2005. I can't even begin to imagine what it was like before that. Life in Bihar is easily still the most primitive of anywhere I've been. This was where any thought of India as simply a holiday destination fell away; there was no escaping the personal meaning held in this landscape. 'I am from here,' I thought over and over. This refrain ran through my head on a loop the entire time I was in Bihar.

Women had seemed strangely absent in Delhi; here they were everywhere. It was all I could do not to stare. I fought the urge to turn my head to catch every detail as we passed by. Barefoot, they marched down the road or worked the land, washed the clothes and tended to the animals, often accompanied by children. Being a woman in this place must be grim: constant, grinding work. I had tried my best to be inconspicuous, wearing the baggiest, dullest clothing I'd brought with me, and donning an Indian shawl. I was only wearing a fraction of the make-up I'd usually wear at home and left my hair largely to its own devices but I still stuck out like a sore thumb. There was something about my relatively groomed state that made me feel feeble, flimsy, timorous even, compared to the women here and the strength they exuded. It was a paradox: I couldn't have felt more out of place, and yet here was where I should have belonged.

It took us almost six hours to drive the 187 kilometres; Nitish Kumar's upgrades still have some way to go. Graham and I talked very little. Both of us were struck by the poverty. Graham had visited Africa before and was better prepared for the absolute poverty. I'd had no such preparation.

Every time we found ourselves stuck in a tiny village waiting for a truck to creep through the narrow streets with just millimetres of clearance between the vehicle and the overhanging roofs, I would search all the faces I could see: the children, the men, but mostly the women. I had spent so many years in wilful ignorance about this place, but now I wanted to know every story. I wanted to ask every woman how she survived, hear what brought her happiness and what prompted despair. I wanted to hear from every child about their upbringing, their schooling, their dreams and what they thought of the world. I wanted to know every single tiny, trivial detail of their daily lives, because they were lives that could so easily have been mine. The scale of the poverty shocked and sickened me. How easily would a person, no matter how capable or full of potential, sink into the dust here. How many tens of millions has it happened to even since I was born? Why was I the fortunate one, plucked out of this life into something so different?

As we passed more subsistence farms and straw huts, everyday words like 'tough' were completely redefined. And my mind turned to 'interest rate day' in Australia.' On the first Tuesday of every month, the Reserve Bank board meets to set the official interest rate. It drives me bonkers at the best of times: the countdown some media run in the minutes leading up to the announcement, the rush by every journalist and news outlet to publish the board's decision one second faster than any other. Australians are obsessed with these decisions, part of our obsession with owning property. Any interest rate rise is accompanied by stories about the mortgage holders who will now be 'doing it tough'. In front of my eyes that phrase had been brought to life. The people of Bihar were doing it tough, just as they did every day. I vowed never again to use that phrase unless it was really justified.

Ramesh barely communicated during the drive; he was concentrating on his task. I studied the back of his thin frame, his serious demeanour. I wondered what he thought of Graham and me, especially me with my Indian looks but foreign ways. I wondered where he lived and where he would stay during our time in Bettiah. Could he read? Did he know how to find somewhere to stay? Did he feel our presence as a weight, his responsibility not only to drive but also to protect these two naive westerners? Could he feel my fear?

On the Mahatma Gandhi Setu Bridge out of Patna he had turned to us and indicated that we needed to pay a government toll. It was under a hundred rupees (less than two Australian dollars). As we went further into the countryside we came several times upon what might be called improvised tolls: young boys on the road stopping cars and insisting they pay up before they could proceed. The boys were so young it didn't seem very threatening, but I wasn't about to risk refusing. Remembering my doctor's advice, we just paid. They were asking for 20 rupees—a few cents for me, a meal for them.

It was almost dark by the time we reached Bettiah. Smoke from the fires outside the huts along the road mixed with the early evening fog, and by five o'clock it was impossible to distinguish how much of the haze was fog and how much smoke. The acrid smell crept into the car even though all the windows were wound up. Fluorescent lights flicked on at the stalls and roadside stands they had instead of shops. I didn't see any electrical light coming from the huts. We entered the city via the dustiest, narrowest and rockiest road so far. If anything, it looked even worse than what I'd seen in the video. The buildings were so dilapidated they must have been defying physics to remain standing. My overactive imagination went into hyperdrive. All I could think about was my biological mother living here as a teenager. Was she scared as she made her way along these streets? Was she dragged into and then raped in one of the dark lanes and alleys we passed? Was that how I came to be?

In the dark the city was terrifying, and we had no idea how to get to St Mary's, the former orphanage at Fakirana. Ramesh stopped to ask a couple of people, without much success. In India it's considered polite to give some help, even if you have no idea of the answer to the question. Commonly locals will just wave you further down the street, taking you no nearer to your destination. That's what happened to us, although finally the words 'St Mary's' got us to a Catholic church in the centre of the city. With trepidation I got out, left Graham in the car with Ramesh and our gear, and walked down an unlit passage to the side door.

Once again I was knocking on a complete stranger's door, this time in the dark and far away from anyone who spoke English. It wasn't the right place. The men inside tried to help but we couldn't understand each other and resorted to vague hand gestures. I went back to the car no wiser. We had done so well in getting so far safely. The orphanage couldn't be far—knowing it was nearby but inaccessible because I couldn't communicate with anyone was excruciatingly frustrating.

Using the universal approach of raising his voice to speak to someone in another language, Ramesh turned around to Graham and me, trying once more to see if there was some word that would unlock the navigational maze that confronted us. Apart from the raised voice, he was incredibly patient. I was vibrating with tension. All I could think about was that I had finally made it here, to Bettiah, and now we were going to be robbed and kidnapped.

Then I had a brainwave: Sister Smigta in Delhi had told us that she'd been posted here originally. She would know how to direct us, or at least the words we'd need to use to ask a local. She'd given us her mobile number before we left Holy Cross. We might not have 3G for data, but we still had a phone signal. I dialled up her number, and thankfully the call connected. I explained our situation and handed the phone to Ramesh. She gave him directions, and after our earlier forty minutes of driving aimlessly around Bettiah it only took us another ten minutes to reach the gates to the compound where I had been an orphanage baby.

Finally we had made it to Fakirana, and I have never felt such sheer, utter relief as I did when we entered those gates. The guard sat in a small hut at the entrance; it was dark and foggy, and the driveway and entrance of the brightly painted main building were lit up. I remember the light as being warm, even though most of India's internal lighting that I saw was of the white fluoro, energy-saving kind.

Fakirana is a complex made up of a series of buildings, with the main four outlining an internal square grassy courtyard. A covered walkway ten metres or so long connected the main building where the sisters lived with a parallel structure that served as guest rooms.

Ramesh parked on the edge of the grassy courtyard. A slim nun strode forward, looking slightly concerned, perhaps because we were by now an hour later than expected, but obviously happy to see us. She introduced herself as Sister Lissil and welcomed us in. She was pleased we'd arrived safely and chatted with Ramesh about the journey. I had wondered to Graham in the car where Ramesh would stay, but Sister Lissil provided the answer even before we could put the question to her, offering him a room and getting it all organised right away. Just minutes later she was showing Graham and me to our room.

Now I understood why I couldn't find a hotel. They didn't exist in the ways a westerner would expect. I guessed for Ramesh that he would have been able to find himself a room somewhere if he'd had to but there was no way we would have even known where to start. During our email exchanges I had asked Sister Lissil for a recommendation and she had instead invited us to stay at Fakirana. As I now saw, the former orphanage looked like a luxury hotel compared to what was outside the gates. Even so, from the outside, the buildings reminded me of spooky old mental asylums in American movies.

Inside, steel beds sat high off the floor with frames for the mosquito nets. The bathroom was big and basic with a shower with a cold tap only, a small ceramic sink and a toilet. But right now it felt like paradise. We hadn't broken for a toilet stop the entire journey; I decided I'd rather leave to my imagination the sort of 'toilet' one might find on the journey to Bettiah. There are things India has taught me to never again take for granted, and toilets are one of them. I now have much more appreciation for the significance of 19 November, which the United Nations has designated World Toilet Day, to focus on the consequences faced by those (especially women and children) who don't have access to a clean sanitation facility. The UN says 2.5 billion people do not have access to hygienic amenities including toilets. Years later I travelled to the United Nations for the first time to report on Australia's role as temporary President of the Security Council (an important body which rules on international conflicts and disputes.) A giant toilet was outside for World Toilet Day. I instantly thought of Bihar as I stood waiting in the boardroom of the General Secretary Ban Ki-moon's office. Forget the Empire State and Chrysler buildings, memories of straw-thatched outhouses came to mind instead. Returning to where I came from would prove to be unforgettable, even though I only spent two days at Fakirana—my first true home. Those first moments in our room were incredibly emotional.

I looked around. A wooden cupboard sat against one concrete wall of our room, and against another was a tiny table with a vase of flowers and a place card wishing us a 'hearty welcome'. I smiled through welling tears. Happiness glowed from that piece of paper in what initially felt like the unhappiest of settings. Feeling overwhelmed, I sat down on the bed. The mattress was so thin I could feel the steel springs through the foam padding.

I suddenly felt overcome with grief—for everything I'd seen on the journey here; for the mother I'd never known. I felt sickened by the possibility that she might be somewhere close by, potentially suffering or living a merciless life, while I knew at the end of this I would be jetting back to the everyday luxuries of life in Australia—where I'd never had cause before to feel grateful for a clean toilet. I had imagined what Bihari life might be like but the reality outdid any portrait I might have visualised. The picture of what I had narrowly missed out on was now clearer but horrifying. I see-sawed between feeling gratitude and guilt. Gratitude that this wasn't my life but then guilt for all the suffering poverty caused for others. For Sister Lissil's sake I fought my desire to curl up on the bed and sob. She was expecting us to wash and appear for dinner, and that's what we did.

Thank goodness for the sisters and their positive energy. Within minutes we were talking, smiling and joking. The accommodation might have looked cold and institutional at first glance but these women had a warm magnetism and were unexpectedly hilarious. It felt good, indeed humbling, to be in the presence of such strong, dynamic women. The rest of the evening shone, the fog couldn't have felt further away. The night ended in many shared laughs, especially when Ramesh arrived back from his meal in town lively and animated. The change from a serious, quiet lad into this bubbly gent didn't escape Lissil's sharp eyes. 'I think you have taken the drink,' she said mischievously, pretending to knock back an invisible bottle.

Ramesh held both hands up in front of his chest, palms facing outwards. 'Nahi, Sister,' he said over and over, an enormous grin on his face. It was a lovely moment. Even though I understood barely a word he spoke, it was easy to detect the respectful way he addressed her. We gently teased Ramesh a little more and my stomach hurt from laughing. Lissil translated our thanks to him for his careful and safe driving and then sent us all to bed before the generators shut down for the night just after nine o'clock.

The next morning when we awoke and peered out the door, we saw Ramesh sitting in the fog just outside. He jumped up and darted across to us, holding out his phone. Eventually we understood that we needed to call Vikas back. He had called to check in and make sure we were okay and that Ramesh had driven safely. We assured Vikas on both fronts. I wanted to tell Ramesh to relax, chill out, wind down, sleep in, but I didn't have the words. I constantly found myself feeling guilty at the eager and ultra-hospitable service Indians provided. Western guilt.

Right in front of our room, in one half of the grassy court-yard, was an empty sandpit, dotted with a few steel rocking toys, a metal seesaw and some half-sunken tyres, next to a huge jackfruit tree. For some reason I instantly pictured Damian in the play area, even though he was just nine months old when he was adopted and if this sandpit had even existed then he could have done little more than sit upright in it. To me that banged-up outdoor play setting spoke powerfully of all the children who had been here, in this orphanage. It had a haunting aspect to it. There was a depth of feeling in the air. I felt it the moment I first glimpsed that little playground through the fog, and it didn't go away until we were back on the road to Patna.

We had a delicious breakfast and I asked if the sisters had kept any records from my time here. Lissil smiled and nodded knowingly; she had clearly been expecting my question. After breakfast, she assured us, we'd have a look at the record book.

The Fakirana book was just like Delhi's version. A piece of Damian and me was recorded here too—a page for me, a page for my brother. I felt the same delight I'd experienced in Delhi, poring over the book that contained the scant details of our time in Fakirana. But it felt even more significant, tangible and meaningful here in Bettiah, knowing that these walls had heard our first baby gurgles and cries.

Just as I had in Delhi, I took a pen and updated our contact details. On both pages, I updated the columns headed

'Progress' with the entry 'very good progress'. It was a lovely experience to be able to provide a bookend to our beginnings. I also felt a sense of gratitude that this trip wasn't a quest for missing information, prompted by a need to fill in the details about myself that I had never known. If it had been, I would have been sorely disappointed. There was no more information here than I already knew. But it was enough for me to just see the book, to know that I'd been here. No longer was India something that I could hold apart from who I was.

We talked about all the countries to which children from Fakirana had been adopted. As well as Australia there was the United States, France, Switzerland, and many others. Hesitantly, I said, 'You know, I don't really feel Indian . . .' I faltered to a halt, wondering if this was my worst faux pas yet. 'Of course you don't,' one of the sisters replied straight away. 'You are Australian.'

And that was the true start of the permanent, monumental change in my relationship with India. I felt a lightness, a sense of freedom to truly accept this place as part of my story but not my sole identity. All at once I felt as though a rusted or stuck gear I had been trying over and over to move had just clicked into place. It was as simple as that.

We sat on the verandah that ran along the front of the main building and talked about the nuns' experiences, with the current generation welcoming 'home' the children who'd been nurtured and adopted out by the previous generations.

It struck me how rich a history this place had. Just as I'd felt when visiting old castles in the United Kingdom, I now wished these walls could talk. I wished they could tell me the stories of the nuns, the children, and of the parents and other family members who brought them here, hoping they'd be given new and rich lives with loving families either in India or abroad. In the very early years of the orphanage, the nuns had raised the children to live with them, but they soon realised that no matter how much they loved them, the children needed families of their own.

There were only two sisters from the old days whose names I knew and so could ask about, and I already knew that Sister Hermann-Josef from Delhi had died long ago. When we were growing up Mum would always speak very lovingly of her and tell us how much she wished we could meet her but that she'd already died. The nuns told me that Sister Gratia, the nun from Fakirana who had corresponded with Mum, was very old and living down south. I also learned that there was only about a fifteen-year window in which the sisters had operated the orphanage—either side of that and Damian and I would have missed out.

While it was a shock to them at first, the sisters said they have now become used to the orphanage's children coming 'home' as adults. It had never occurred to them that we would, but people have come back from all around the world. Some speak French, others English; few understand Hindi. Some of course will never return, for many different reasons. The ones that do have mostly been happy in their lives, but one of the nuns, in her eighties, took me aside later in the morning and, squeezing my hand, told me about some who'd come back deeply troubled. Some were alcoholics or drug addicts. For them adoption had not been a happy experience. 'Are you happy?' she asked me.

'Completely,' I replied. I didn't need to feign my conviction. But I did feel doubly blessed, first to have been adopted, and to be happily so. What an indiscriminate lottery I had won.

In the morning sunlight, Fakirana looked very different and cheery with its pastel coloured green, blue and pink exteriors. What had been an orphanage was now a training centre for young nuns, a school for deaf children from all over the state, a place for local young girls to learn to read and write, and a home for the elderly, disabled, mentally ill and destitute. The residents lived in the wing adjacent to the row of rooms where we were staying. Their beds were hammock-like slings and the rooms looked out onto the grassed areas. Some of the disabled residents could barely communicate. The sisters cared for them, as they explained, to give these people some dignity in what was often their final days or months. Where would they be if not for Fakirana? My impressions from seeing Bettiah the night before left me sick with anguish at the thought that they would otherwise be lying in some alleyway waiting to die.

The lessons from my Catholic upbringing about what it meant to be a Christian were transformed into real, practical meaning at Fakirana. It was literally the place where the poor's feet were washed and those that society had left behind were taken in and embraced. The place pulsated with purpose.

The young deaf children who would normally have been there were on holiday, but we were taken into a room full of local girls learning the basics of reading and writing. Some looked as young as ten, others sixteen or seventeen. The nuns introduced Graham and me to the class, explaining that I'd been there as a baby, and translated the girls' questions. They knew very little about Australia—just the existence of kangaroos. They wanted to know what I did and how old I was. They sang and danced as we clapped and laughed and mimed silly jokes.

What did their future hold? I wondered. At most, these girls would learn how to count and read some basic passages of text. Even in 2012, none were likely to leave their hometowns or receive any further education. They would marry, have children, and raise their families. At their age I already knew that I would be a journalist and that I wanted to travel and above all learn as much as I could about the world around me: its politics, its people, its natural history, its languages, its cultures. For me the world was always an infinite encyclopaedia and I wanted to devote my life to understanding as much of it as I could first-hand. That thirst had been within me for years, since I was at least as young as these girls, who lit up the classroom with their gorgeous and warm innocent smiles. I wanted to give them everything I'd had, all the hopes and educational opportunities that Australia had given me. It was an impossible dream. I left their classroom smiling, but with tears in my eyes.

Graham and I trekked around the grounds, which stretched over several acres. It was an almost self-sustaining community. The sisters sold their surplus fruits and vegetables, and the only food they ate that wasn't produced on site was the meat they bought in town. They sowed wheat, which was harvested and ground into flour for naan. Old fruit trees that in season bore mangoes and jackfruit towered overhead. We saw fields of potato, pea and tomato crops. The nuns also kept cows for fresh milk, pigs, and horses in stables. They employed a full-time farmhand to tend to it all, and extra workers were brought in from the town for gardening and harvesting at busy times.

Particularly striking was a vivid yellow field of flowers. I wondered if the crop was canola, which I'd seen when I was growing up in Bathurst and which also has a bright yellow flower. But it turned out they were mustard plants. The nuns told us it was common for babies to be kept warm simply by rubbing a little mustard onto their skin. Aha! I thought; now I knew what had suddenly kicked in to allow me to eat whole chillies with ease. These funny little connections had such an impact on me. I had never minded not looking like Mum and Dad or being able to join in when Dominic, Gabriela and Joseph discussed which cousin they resembled. But I did appreciate the snippets of understanding I gained about my personal history in India. It turned out to matter after all.

Tucked right down the back at the furthest point of the property was a cemetery where tiny babies who didn't make it to adoption were buried. No, I wasn't doubly blessed; make it triply blessed, I thought, turning away, choked with sadness.

The highlight of the entire visit was seeing the building where we babies had been kept when the orphanage was running. The fourth of the buildings surrounding the internal courtyard, it now held just a few traces of the little lives that had once passed through it. There were two main rooms where we would have been cared for as babies; one of them was now a chapel for the nuns. Walking into the building, with the knowledge that I had been there, cried there, been looked after within these four walls so far away from everything I knew, was a hallowed experience. It was a similar feeling to that I've had walking into grand cathedrals—St Paul's, Westminster Abbey, Notre-Dame, St Vitus—except that this was far more precious. I found I adopted the same reverent tone as I had in those religious monuments. In fact, where I might have tried to snap a sneaky photo on my iPhone in the Abbey, say, the image of that room remains in my memory only. It was too sacred to photograph.

As I looked around in the complete silence, it was easy to try to listen out for a distant echo of the babies' cries and imagine the nuns rushing between rooms. My overriding thought, standing in that room, was that I knew I had been there before, I could *feel* it. The feeling was overpowering and tremendous.

When the centre had stopped operating as an orphanage, the nuns gave away their baby things to those in need—all but one relic, a white swinging cot kept on the balcony. At seeing it, my cheeks almost burst with my smile of delight; I knew without doubt that I had been put in there. Other returnees who were there as babies have apparently felt the same way. The sisters laughingly told us that one lady tried to jump right back in, never mind that she was thirty years old!

In the afternoon we asked Ramesh to drive us into town. The sisters wanted to pick up some goods at the local store and offered to take me to the marketplace in case I wanted to buy some local souvenirs. Ramesh fussed over the sisters. He chatted with them and asked about my Indian looks and why Graham and I had wanted to come to Bettiah.

The city looked far less frightening by day but still wretchedly poor. With the nuns in their dusty pink saris as our guides, we were welcomed with smiles. It was obvious that they were well regarded in society, which is no surprise given how prominent religion is in India. The nuns took us to their regular stalls and were welcomed with warm, familiar greetings. There were none of the touts who had plagued our every step in Delhi. I bought some shawls, thicker, itchier and woollier than the ones I'd found in Delhi. I made sure I bought one for Mum and one for Melissa—I knew they would want their own piece of Bettiah.

After shopping we stopped by a high-walled centre near the local hospital and met some more Holy Cross sisters, who nursed at the local hospital. They asked about my life in Australia and whether I'd wear the shawls that I'd bought in India. Yes, I think so, I told them, smiling. And I meant it. I was a long way from the girl who had shuddered at any mention of India.

As we moved around the town I realised I was intently focused on the women. They were beautiful. Tall and slender, they moved purposefully among the traffic of trucks, cars, goats, bicycles, motorbikes and cows. I've never seen anyone glide more elegantly than Bihar's women. They were usually carrying something on their head: a load of sticks, a container of water, vegetables, fruit, anything that needed to be transported. Brilliant saris formed vertical slashes of hot pinks, burnt oranges and baby blues. But it was their faces I couldn't stop looking at. Angular and dominated by prominent cheekbones, they looked purposeful. I found myself searching every woman's face we passed, trying to spot my own features in hers. Could she still be out there after all, my mother? She would be forty-two. I tried to focus on women of around that age, but I found ages almost impossible to guess there. Still, I couldn't stop trying the whole time I was in Bihar.

As we arrived back at the Fakirana centre, we saw a group of girls lined up in the main garden. They were flashes of colour in their loose, flowing *shalwar kameez* tops and pants, moving in rhythm as they followed the instructor in front of them. I was taken by the sight. 'What are they doing?' I asked.

Karate, explained one of the sisters. 'It's another form of empowerment, along with reading and writing,' she said. 'It will help them protect themselves if, when they go back to their families, they are married to a man who turns out to be abusive.' These nuns floored me. On so many levels they were quietly making an immense difference in the lives of the young women and girls around them.

The sisters' capacity to give seemed endless. Graham, an avid cook and devotee of Indian food, had been delighted earlier by a tour of the giant kitchen. The nuns had asked his favourite food and he'd replied tandoori chicken. That evening as we sat down to dinner, in wafted the smell of chicken cooked in a tandoor. Australia and India were playing each other in a cricket Test match, so we spent much of the evening discussing the scores and the current form of each team. While the sisters had a television and a computer, Lissil received the scores via a text message service. I loved the sight of her stealing a look at her phone, retrieved from somewhere in her sari, for the latest update.

That night I had the strangest experience. I'm a regular and vivid dreamer who can usually remember most of the roaming of my subconscious the next morning. But this was unlike any dream I've had before or since. I'd had trouble getting to sleep because I was so cold. I layered up some of the woollen shawls I'd bought earlier that day, but when even that didn't work, I drew back the mosquito net that separated our steel beds and huddled closer to Graham for his body heat. For the rest of the night I drifted in and out of sleep and at one point fell into the strangest dream.

Although I believe in God and in an afterlife of some indefinable sort, I have never been a huge subscriber to the mystical or supernatural. But in this dream I was back in that room as a baby, staring up at a green and white light. Nothing else happened, but I was pervaded by the certainty that what I was experiencing wasn't a dream at all, but a memory. 'I was here, I remember,' I thought in my dream, and when I woke up I remembered every detail.

I have never felt so certain of anything as I was that I had just experienced a genuine memory from long before the age when children are supposed to be able to make permanent memories. While I was looking around the orphanage, my mind had been saying over and over, 'I was here,' and now it felt as though my subconscious had found a memory to show me. It was a vivid connection and I felt a stronger sense of myself than I'd ever had before. It suddenly became easy to just accept who I was, what I had been and what I would always be. There was nothing to fight anymore.

Over and over the sisters at Fakirana had told me that the place was my 'first home'. Initially I thought they were just being polite and welcoming, but by the time we were ready to leave I felt the truth of it in a way I could never have imagined a few years earlier. Fakirana is all about roots: the roots of the sustaining trees and plants; the roots of the women and the relationships, care and nourishment they provide. For decades, this place has been the original root for so many lives now branched far and wide across the globe . . . mine included.

8

PRIDE, LOVE AND GRATITUDE

We left the sisters of Fakirana the next morning after breakfast. Our one regret was that before we left Delhi we'd withdrawn only around ten thousand rupees from an ATM, not liking to carry too much cash on us. We had spent some and needed a little more for the journey back, but we gave the nuns the six or seven thousand rupees that were left. (We hadn't found anywhere to withdraw money in Bettiah.) We wished we'd brought much, much more.

During our time there, Graham and I had discussed a meaningful and lasting way we could contribute to Fakirana once we got back home. As we left, ever generous, he told the sisters to contact us when they wanted to proceed with a project they'd mentioned they had in mind, to retrofit the place with a solar-powered system for better ventilation in the hot months. We'd figured the heat must be excruciating in summer and would do what we could to fix that.

Whereas on the way to Bettiah I had been swamped by anxiety and Graham and I were largely silent, on the drive back to Patna I was much calmer. I was still engrossed by the scenes passing by outside the car window but we chatted too. We were both full of wonder at everything we saw. The experience of living was a complete rewrite of everything I had ever known. I appreciated that to be Indian was one thing, to be Bihari was another.

In Patna we farewelled Ramesh. While waiting for our flight back to Delhi we thought we'd try our luck at one of the restaurants in the airport complex. It was nothing special, just a hole in the wall type restaurant with a few tables and a drinks fridge. And that was all we needed for an Indian feast. We sat down next to a group of three young Australians who were backpacking around the country and had made it all the way to Bihar. As soon as we heard one another's accents we introduced ourselves and swapped travel recommendations.

Oddly, that meal in that funny little unkempt shop is still, several years and many trips later, one of the best meals we've had in India. Unlike some of the restaurants we'd tried in Delhi at the hotel's recommendation, where we found the food bland and a little boring, the cooks here hadn't westernised the food one bit. It was bursting with flavour, heat and complexity. The total cost was about four dollars for a couple of curries with delicious bread. This is what I found myself loving about India: the things that wowed were often the unexpected and unplanned experiences.

We arrived back in Delhi with a sense of relief. Not only was the hard part over, but our trip to Bihar had been hugely fulfilling. I felt changed, like I was now a part of it all. Not that I belonged exactly; I was still Australian, after all. But I felt totally at ease here with the apparent contradiction of my brown skin and Aussie accent. Everyone else seemed to be.

We were ready to have fun. And top of our list was visiting Agra to see the Taj Mahal. I hadn't organised a single thing for this part of the trip, so we asked the concierge at the Imperial the best way of getting there. He recommended a day trip leaving on the early morning train. We felt comfortable now about getting around on our own and wanted to experience India's famous railway system, so a couple of days after our return from Bihar, we got up before dawn and headed back to the central railway station where we had been for the Salaam Baalak tour. (Now knowing that they sheltered there, I looked around for street children but couldn't see any.) The train trip was a breeze. The best part was the chai wallahs coming through the carriages to sell hot milky tea, calling out, 'Chai, chai.'

The difference between Agra and Delhi was apparent from the moment we stepped off the train. While the old part of Delhi is crowded and grubby and full of life, the new part of the city is reminiscent of Canberra, with its wide avenues, diplomatic enclaves and planned symmetry. Agra is something else again. The fact that it's on the itinerary of pretty much every tourist to India hasn't led to it becoming sanitised. Industrial smog chokes the air and has corroded the Taj over the years; scooters are piled with up to nine family members, including babies; aggressive monkeys run wild; water buffalo block the streets at will; and poverty is in your face at every turn.

The touts were out in force, of course, thrusting food and armfuls of flowers and cheap necklaces and anything else they thought a tourist might want at us as we walked out to find our cab. But we kept back and were able to make our way to the quaintly labelled 'Pri-paid taxi' stand unencumbered. Having booked a car and driver I could sit back and relax, ready to enjoy being a tourist for the day instead of an adoptee. But then a stranger slid into the front passenger seat next to the driver. He turned and grinned broadly, introducing himself as Sanjay. 'Oh Lord,' I thought, 'another bloody Bobby.'

How wrong I was. Sanjay, it turned out, was an officially registered guide. Qualifying to become a guide can take years. They must pass written and oral exams and they usually speak half a dozen languages. Sanjay was an absolute gem; as I later discovered, his fellow guides are almost universally terrific. In fact, they are easily the best thing about touring India. Despite being part of a government-run program, Sanjay's services didn't have a set fee. 'Pay me what you think I've been worth at the end of the day,' he said when we pressed him. It sounded like a recipe for scamming, but when the time came we were happy to pay handsomely—he had earned every rupee.

Mum had come back from India underwhelmed by the Taj. I find this hard to fathom. For me, the 'monument to love' was breathtaking. It did take forever to tour, with a long, snaking queue of sightseers. Fortunately, having arrived on the early side, we were close to the front of the line. Even so, the time it took to make our way to the entrance, abandon shoes for fibrous slippers and actually get inside provided the opportunity for Sanjay to give us a crash course in Indian medieval history, something I knew not one skerrick about.

He explained that the Taj Mahal was built by Mughal emperor Shah Jahan in the 1600s for his beloved wife Mumtaz Mahal, who had died giving birth to their fourteenth child. This adoration of a wife was unusual given the Mughals had multiple wives. And their harems of concubines, female relatives, children, servants, ladies in waiting and guards could number into the thousands. On his death, Shah Jahan was buried alongside Mumtaz inside the Taj— the monument of love he had built for her. It wasn't just the inside, the magnificent dome or even the famed symmetry of the building that wowed us. It was the intricate inlay of semi-precious stones carved into the marble forming beautiful strands of flowers. The carving work was ornate and you knew you were standing in a one of a kind.

After we'd gone through the building we went back out into the grounds. It was mid-morning and the lines had swelled tenfold. Still, no one was impatient or in a rush. Foreigners happily paid a bit more to enter than the locals, as they do at most of the country's famed sites. Watching the variety of tourists, Japanese, Chinese, Indian, Australian, American, European, take in the splendour gave the feeling of truly being in the centre of the old and new worlds.

Wandering out through the terraces allowed us to really take in the juxtaposition of this exquisite marble creation with the ugliness surrounding it. The Yamuna river (an offshoot of the Ganges), which runs behind the Taj, is heavily polluted. In the late 1990s, the government set up strict emissions controls from coal factories within a 10,000-square-kilometre zone around the monument, and restricted cars from travelling within 500 metres of the Taj. The controls led to the factories across the river being abandoned, but the air is still often thick, as smoke from the Hindu crematorium just down from the great dome mingles with the city's general pollution.

Gazing from the Persian minarets to the derelict factory smokestacks, it struck me that Agra was emblematic of India as a whole: great beauty, lavish remains of opulence and wealth from times gone by, and magnificence to rival the legacy of old empires around the world, all choking under the pressures of modern life. And yet it made no claims to being anything other than what it was. As I stood in front of the Taj, something new jolted me. I recognised this unfamiliar feeling pumping through my chest as pride. Marvelling at the tourists for hundreds of metres, Indians and foreigners alike, flocking to see this wonder, I realised it was mine if I wanted it. All this time, India had been there for me to come and claim if I chose to. I was ready.

As India offered itself up to me, I suddenly heard in my memory the voice of the woman in the visa office in Canberra, with her comment about my 'next trip' to India. I'd thought the idea ridiculous then, but now I knew she was right: there would be a next time. I was sure as hell getting that former citizens visa, I vowed to myself as I stood in the gardens, turning back to gape at the Taj. In fact, Graham and I made a vow to come back every year. I had never felt so certain about anything as I did about the affinity, the new love I felt for this magnificent country that had waited so patiently for me to grow up.

The blossoming that began in my heart in that moment came to full flower just a few minutes later when Sanjay led us across to Agra Fort. While the Taj's majesty is awe-inspiring, it's in Agra Fort that India's history really comes alive.

The fort is actually a walled city comprised of palaces, and was founded in the 1500s by one of India's most celebrated leaders, Akbar the Great (Shah Jahan's grandfather). Like England's famed castles, its structures hint at countless and astounding stories of extravagance, debauchery and political intrigue. Sanjay told us that beginning with their third leader, Akbar, the Mughals who ruled Hindustan, as it was known, made Agra, not Delhi, their capital. Akbar, a Muslim, promoted religious tolerance; he was greatly interested in other faiths, encouraging regular discussions and debates between religious leaders of the time. Growing up, I had never heard of Akbar, or even Shah Jahan and Mumtaz. When we'd studied great and terrible leaders of history, we looked towards Britain, Europe and the Americas. I had never realised that India's history was full of brilliant, gory, depraved and visionary leaders to rival anything in the west.

Showing us the lotus flowers, Hindu symbols and Star of David carved into the entryway of the fort, Sanjay explained that they were there to demonstrate the Mughals' tolerance for the various faiths of their wives. He pointed out the hollowed interiors through which water would be pumped during the hot seasons—medieval air conditioning! But it was the harem and the underground prison for misbehaving members of the harem that completely gripped me. How on earth could I not have known about a ruler with a harem of between four and five thousand women? Yet look how much attention was given to Henry VIII with his paltry six wives.

Sanjay guided us to a balcony overlooking what was now a very carefully manicured square of grass, like a private courtyard. It was here that the Mughal rulers would hold markets for the eligible women of Agra. In theory, the women came to buy and sell jewels, but if their own sparkle caught the ruler's eye they'd be admitted to the harem, never to leave. The original meat market, I thought. One can only imagine the politics in a five-thousand-strong harem. The more I heard, the more amazed I was that these stories aren't better known outside of India. Remembering back to my early obsession with America, home of 'the western', I wondered why so much of the world was ignorant of these eastern stories.

(When I returned home I raided online bookstores for writings on the history of the Mughals. The architecture, the politics, the wars, the loves: it all fascinated me. Many of these books noted that the five-thousand-strong harem in Agra actually included all sorts of subsidiary staff; the ruler had plenty of lovers, but not quite five thousand of them. Before our trip to India, I would never have imagined that so many of these books would soon sit on my shelves alongside my favourite publications on Tudor history and modern politics. But now I wanted to learn everything I could about these societies and how they operated.)

Our day in Agra was broken up with several mandatory stops at marble factories, gem stores and rug mills aimed at promoting local craftsmanship. Much of the jewellery and many of the carpets and marble inlays echoed, or paid homage to, the designs and patterns featured in the medieval structures dotted around the city. Inside a rug store we met an elderly man transforming Australian merino wool into a patterned carpet via tiny individual knots woven on a loom nearly as tall as him. It was a characteristically Persian-inspired pattern, with colourful life-size winding flower motifs, all created from the memories he held in his head. I was reminded of Ramesh, driving all through Bihar, not being able to read a single sign but relying on his natural instincts of observation to guide him and never once making a mistake. If we ever go back to Fakirana I'll seek him out and ask him to drive us again, knowing that once he had taken a route he would remember it forever.

I walked back to the car transformed. The six or so hours we had spent at the Taj and Agra Fort had triggered a fundamental change in the way I saw myself and my place in the world. I realised I didn't have to fight so hard to prove that I belonged to Australia: I did and I always would. But that didn't mean rejecting the country of my birth. At last I accepted the truth: India really was part of me and I was part of it. Fakirana had given me the freedom to accept India. Agra gave me the reason to love it. Knowing how much I love history, I shouldn't have been surprised that I would adore Agra so much, but it had never occurred to me that this famous, historic symbol of love would open the floodgates of my love for India.

We finished the day at a gem store and I bought a few little necklace pendants that would look nice on TV when I got back to Australia and went back to work. I wanted to Indianise my Australian life. I laughed to hear myself say it (lucky that Mum had taught us to be experts in laughing at ourselves!). The gem-store owner was unlike most vendors in India in that he didn't lay on the hard sell. We ended up buying a few more pieces than we would have otherwise, simply because we appreciated his approach so much. So we were startled to see him tearing up the platform, mobile EFTPOS machine in hand, as we waited for our train back to Delhi. He breathlessly told us he had mistakenly charged us seven hundred rupees instead of seven thousand. Ordinarily, I might have suspected a scam, but my intuition told me he was legit. Given that we'd paid on credit card we figured we could always make a claim if it turned out we'd been dudded. We hadn't. I felt for him. All his hard work to make sure we bought something and the fear he must have felt when he realised he'd practically given us his pieces for free!

Both Graham and I felt liberated on the train ride back. We each felt as though we'd been set free to embrace and love the country. Graham had needed a lot less convincing than me, of course, but it was important, if we were going to come back, that we both felt the same way.

We also now felt confident to see as much of Delhi as we could on our own. In our final few days in the city, we caught as many tuk-tuks as we could and bargained for fun rather than for deals. We ticked off visits to the impressive Red Fort, soaring Qutab Minar and Humayun's historic tomb. And we finally tried some delicious street food (with interesting results on the flight home).

We also did one more walking tour. I'd looked it up after returning from Bihar—it was the most highly recommended thing to do in Delhi on TripAdvisor. It was run by a man called Dhruv, a wealthy Indian businessman who had lived in America. His mission was to show westerners Delhi beyond the dirt and poverty. Dhruv picked Graham and me up from the Imperial and took us to the city's famed Chandni Chowk market, where we met the two others who were taking the tour that day, one a Swedish businessman in his early fifties, the other an Englishman a bit older than me.

The tours were clearly well known to the locals. As we wound our way through the back streets of Old Delhi, we stopped by Dhruv's favoured stalls, sampling curries, fried potatoes and sweets made from caramelised milk. With him as our guide, people were much friendlier and more accommodating.

The cost was forty dollars per person, which by Indian standards was very expensive, but it was the perfect way to see the old part of the city. We called at stores that made wedding invitations, and Dhruv explained to us that some people would spend thousands of dollars (not rupees) on wedding invites alone. Money, he said, was simply spent differently in India than it was in the west and not everyone you saw was poor, even if it looked that way. The position occupied by a tea-seller standing on the road might look ad-hoc to us, but the spot had likely been in his family for generations and might well be a lucrative business.

I accepted this. Appearances were certainly not everything: never judge a book by its cover, right? But after our excellent street tour, culminating with a home-cooked dinner with Dhruv's wife at their very beautiful, big family home, he led us out to his car to drive us back to the hotel. An old man was sleeping in his rickshaw on the side of the road. The night was freezing—literally below zero. I desperately wanted to enjoy Dhruv's Delhi, but the poverty just slapped you in the face as abruptly or as harshly as the beggar children beating against the car window for money.

Even so, we left Delhi on a high and full of love for the country, pledging to return. Graham loved it just as much as I did (and because he is far more patient, possibly even a bit more than me). It was easily the most fascinating place we'd ever visited, and we both wanted to spend the rest of our lives exploring every state, tasting our way between the different regions, and trying to understand the country and its complex people. We had already decided that we'd head overseas to live at some stage within the next five years, with England at the top of our list of destinations. We now put India on that list, too.

Everywhere we went I kept thinking, 'Everyone here probably has a story to tell that should be heard, and as a journalist I could help them tell it.' But I also had to accept that there were stories and attitudes that made me deeply uncomfortable. I keep thinking back to an encounter I had in Delhi not long before we left. I'd been determined to spend every rupee I could before I left India. Central Cottage Industries Emporium is a government-owned chain of stores aimed at cultivating, sustaining and promoting an authentic Indian arts sector, and the flagship Delhi store is next door to the Imperial. It has become a favoured shopping destination of international VIPs for good reason: not only is everything guaranteed to be authentic, but the prices are fixed so there is none of the haggling you have to do on the streets (sure, it can be fun, but it's also exhausting and makes any bit of shopping a long, drawn-out affair).

The store is huge, spread over several floors. You could easily spend a whole day in it, and we did. Buying some silk scarves for my old school friends Rachal and Averil, I began talking to the young man behind the counter. He might have been around my age, though I couldn't be certain. He asked where I was from. Somehow I knew he didn't mean 'What country are you visiting from?', he meant 'Where in India are you from?' It's funny, the question that had enraged me so much in Australia now didn't bother me at all, not since Fakirana.

So I replied, 'I'm from Bihar but was adopted as a baby and I'm Australian.' After visiting there and having such a life-changing experience, I was hankering to talk about it with someone who might know of it. I was in luck: it turned out he was from Bihar too. Our connection made his face light up with a smile. He was from Patna, and he became quieter and sadder as he told me about his father, who had worked in a factory there but lost his arm in a work accident.

He asked what I did for a living. I felt very self-conscious talking about my life in Australia lest it sound like bragging or flaunting my good fortune. I would have preferred to talk about Bihar, to ask him what made the people there happy, what were their aspirations for themselves, their children and their country. Briefly, I told him about my job as a political journalist, which at the time was for the ABC's twenty-four-hour television news channel. He said that ever since his father's accident it had been up to him to provide money for his family. That was why he had come to Delhi, where there was work, and he had to send practically everything he earned back home to Patna. I was uncomfortable. In Australia we don't tend to talk about finances, certainly not with strangers, and when people in India did I was never sure if they were simply sharing facts or if it was supposed to spur me to offer them money. I didn't think that was the intention of the serious man in front of me, to whom I was feeling sympathetic.

But then he asked what caste I was from. I was aghast. It was the first and only time someone had asked me this question in India. I knew little about the caste system, but I realised he was asking in order to place me in a hierarchy. (An Indian girlfriend in Australia jokes that maybe he wanted to marry me, when I tell her this story.) I was incredulous at the question. Had he not heard me say that I was Australian? I felt angry and offended. I finished the transaction and walked away furious, not at him especially, but at everything the conversation had exposed about India. There was fear in the fury too—fear that this country with all its hopes, aspirations and brilliant prospects might never rise above its challenges to be truly magnificent. But perhaps this man wasn't typical after all. I recalled the conversation with my doctor and one of the things she had said in expressing her disgust at Bihar and its 'backwardness': 'Do you know they still believe in the caste system there?' She had spat out the words, her voice full of contempt.

There was so much I still didn't understand about India, and perhaps never would. The place of women here was a prime example. Feminism had taken on a very different meaning for me in this country. I've always been a proud feminist and applauded strong women who have achieved personal success. Women have been the strongest influences in my life: my eldest sister, Melissa, for instance, was someone to look up to and emulate, as were the trio of teachers I revered in high school as my intellectual role models, Trish Stabback, Susan Hayley and Julie Novak. However, like religion, feminism didn't have much of a presence in my everyday life. The way I saw it, it was never really required. My education and my job rewarded my hard work; sexism had never been an enemy I'd had to conquer. I would have been the first to sign on the dotted line if asked to vouch that I believed in the ideals and principles of feminism, but it was hardly a pervasive influence in my day-to-day life. I guess I became a 'lapsed feminist' in much the same way as I would describe myself as a 'lapsed Catholic'.

But visiting India for the first time made me see feminism in a new light. I became obsessed with India's women. Not because of some sense of sisterhood. In fact, rarely did I find them warm or friendly (the nuns not withstanding); much more often they were quite cool and extremely pushy. Dare I say it, they were like myself—very bossy. But there was something about the way they walked through the streets with such strength that drew me to them and made me constantly in awe of them. I see it every time I watch a new documentary or read a story about women in India fighting for respect, recognition, their rights and freedoms. I love being a feisty, independent, exuberant Australian woman, but I blanch at the thought of being a woman in India. On a later trip to Mumbai our guide took us down the city's notorious Red Light District on Falkland Road. The women waited in their tiny holes in the wall. So many of them were there forcibly. It is very common in India for women to be trafficked or their families tricked into sex slavery. I wondered how many village girls from Bihar had been brought to Bombay since I'd been born? I hated to try and guess. 'You can tell the prostitutes by all the loud make-up they wear,' the guide, a male, told us. I was horrified. Most of the women weren't wearing much make-up at all—some looked like they were wearing a fraction of what I'd normally wear at home. If that was loud how did mine look to them? After that I barely wore make-up at all in India. Had the men assumed my painted face meant something else all this time?

There is certainly often a threatening edge to being a woman in Delhi. I found that the men there stared at me and other women in the most intimidating manner. No one I met in India could explain it. You could be wearing the drabbest clothing, have not an inch of flesh showing other than your hands, neck and face, but still they stared as though you were naked. Initially I would acknowledge their gaze and smile back, but there was no response. They just kept on staring, their dark eyes boring holes into me. Soon I learned to keep my eyes down, and it was only when I bought some sunglasses that I felt I could look around undisturbed by their glares. I didn't detect this aggression anywhere else in India; nor did I note the absence of women on the streets anywhere else as I did there. The Delhi gang-rape case, in which a young woman was beaten and raped by six men on a bus and later died from her injuries, happened later that year, in December, and reading about it I was shocked but not surprised.

Women in India face so many barriers just in their day-to-day life. There is a double standard in the value placed on education for boys and girls, for instance, with Indian girls much more likely to miss out than boys. Education is the thing I value most about my upbringing in Australia. With both Mum and Dad being teachers, and Mum in particular loving to read, books had fascinated me from a very early age. I would read anywhere I could: on the bus, walking home; even doing the washing-up I would have my latest book open on the kitchen windowsill in Mum's clear plastic recipe holder.

In 1991, about the time when Mum was first teaching me to read, just one-fifth of Bihari women were literate. I did well at school, not because I was overly brainy or even especially studious, but because learning is something that I adore. But in India I would most likely never have had the opportunity to feed my curious mind.

Now knowing the harsh reality of life for Indian women, it isn't hard to play Sliding Doors and imagine what my life might have been like if I had grown up in Bihar. I would have worked from the earliest possible age. Child labour is outlawed and primary school education is mandatory, but it's up to parents to enrol their children and keep them in school, and many poor rural families believe that the children are of more use if they're put to work. This can mean working long hours farming or, like some boys I saw on the drive from Patna, doing roadworks. I'd had to stop myself from crying out in alarm when I spotted them, aged eight or nine, barefoot and wearing just shorts, laying freshly mixed tar so close to the cars passing at 40 or 50 kilometres an hour that they could have reached out and touched them. The boys were smiling and laughing, so carefree that they could have been building sandcastles instead of laying hot asphalt, but it was a very confronting sight.

Had I grown up poor in Bihar, I'd be able to read and write at a very basic level, if at all; I would have been married while still a girl, become a mother to several children, and I would be working on the land and coming home to a mud-floored, straw-thatched hut. It's hard to comprehend how close I came to that fate, and how many other women are living that life now simply through the accident of their birth.

For as long as I'd known I was adopted, I had understood that there was virtually no information about my biological mother and that there never would be. No name, no history, no explanation even for why I had been given to the orphanage. That she had been practically a child herself, just fourteen when she gave birth to me, was one of the precious few solid facts I had. At an age when I was singing into my hairbrush and slamming the odd door in a teenage tantrum, she was giving birth, probably on a dirt floor.

I didn't think of her often when I was growing up, but when I did my imagination, fed on a diet of novels, ran wild. Very early on I'd concluded that she must have been raped or that she was a prostitute. Why else, I asked myself, would she be having a baby at fourteen? I felt a detached compassion for her, as I would for anyone in those circumstances. She hadn't really known me, I didn't know her, and even if there ever were a way for us to meet, we didn't speak the same language. She was a complete stranger.

At some point over the years I had privately decided that she had probably died. Mum encouraged us to say a prayer for our birth mothers every birthday, and most years I remembered to do so. The framework for me was that fate, destiny, God, Buddha, Shiva, Parvati or whatever you wanted to call it had plucked me from Bettiah and parachuted me right into the middle of the Bourke clan in a country where I could achieve my full potential. I didn't need to find out about my missing mother. I knew that Mum was my mum. Even when we fought, there was never a time when I thought, 'Well, she's not my real mum.' She is my real mum. So I had no longing to meet my biological mother, but I did have a wistful desire to let her know I'd turned out okay; to be able to communicate to her how many opportunities life in Australia had given me. In my birthday prayers I imagined her looking down from heaven, able to see how well my life had worked out.

In truth, for much of the time I was growing up I felt lucky that the information about her was so scant: it closed the door for me. In many ways, I think this was one of the critical elements that made my adoption so successful.

One of the nicest and most touching things anyone ever said to me was about my mother. For some reason, one day when I was seventeen my friend Averil and I were talking about my adoption, within the hearing of my modern history teacher Mrs Stabback. I said how little I knew about my birth mother, and my lovely teacher said to me, 'Well, Latika, one thing you know is that she was smart—because you are.' Because I had so little information about my mother, this was the first thing anyone had ever said that gave me a way to feel genuine pride about what sort of a girl or woman she might have been. Mrs Stabback's generous observation has stayed with me ever since. At the time it gave me great comfort, but after Bihar it also triggers despair. How could an inquisitive mind soar in a place like Bihar if she was giving birth at fourteen years of age?

Even though I really didn't think I would learn anything new, it would have been crazy to go all the way to Fakirana and not ask the sisters if they had any other information or leads on my mother. 'None,' they had said, shaking their heads regretfully. 'We were so busy looking after the babies and getting them into families, we didn't think to keep any records back then. We never thought we'd see those babies coming back wanting to know.' Even so, what they had to tell me changed the ideas I had held about my mother for so many years.

As I learned from them, fourteen was quite a normal age to be giving birth in Bihar back then, because girls were routinely married by that age. I wanted to slap my forehead; I couldn't believe I had never realised that. If I had been interested enough to do any reading about India and the lives of its women prior to my trip, I would have easily discovered this fact for myself. The British first attempted to outlaw child marriage in 1929 but illegal child marriage is still a major scourge afflicting the country. According to the United Nations Population Fund, 'India has one of the highest child marriage prevalence rates in the world.' And the state with the highest percentage of women who are married off before the age of eighteen is Bihar, with 69 per cent fitting that description in 2006. I can accept that it happened in the 1980s, but even having seen Bihar for myself, I am stunned that it still happens on such a staggering scale today when the world is supposed to be making progress in these areas.

But commonplace or not, fourteen is very young for a girl's developing body to have to cope with pregnancy and childbirth, and the sisters said it was likely that my mother had died giving birth to me. If that was so, and my birth father thought he would want to remarry in due course, he would not want to be encumbered by a baby. There's no way of knowing if my biological mother lived in one of those straw huts with cows and goats out the front that dotted every road between Bettiah and Patna. But that was where I pictured her going through the agonies of birthing me on the mud floor.

Was that how I had ended up as one of India's millions of unwanted girls? The UN's Women 2014 report said that the ratio of girl children to boy children in India had 'begun to seriously plummet', showing that the problem is far from improving. In fact, these days the preference for boys is aided by foetal screening and gender-based abortions. In 1981, three years before I was born, the sex ratio in the child population (aged up to six years) in Bihar was quite good, at 981 girls for every 1000 boys. But by 2011 it had declined to 935, according to census figures. The decline is largely led by the urban areas.

The 2013 documentary *It's a Girl*, focusing on 'gender-cide' in India and China, is subtitled: 'The Three Deadliest Words in the World.' The film begins with an Indian woman describing how she had strangled and buried eight of her babies because they were female. As a reviewer in Britain's *Independent* newspaper puts it, 'The brutal irony of femicide is that it is an evil perpetrated against girls by women.' In Bihar now, among a range of measures designed to discourage rural families from neglecting or, worse, killing their baby girls, schoolgirls are given special allowances for uniforms, free books, and a bike when they reach year nine.

The Invisible Girl Project, a US-based not-for-profit organisation which campaigns to change the way India views and values its women and girls, says the gender gap caused by infanticide, gendercide, dowry killings, neglect and violence also leads to women being trafficked—for slavery, sex work or forced marriages. My doctor back in Canberra told me many doctors would end up adopting girl babies abandoned because of their gender.

When I returned home to Australia, my mind still full of India, I went back and raked through each page of correspondence in my orange manila adoption folder. It was magical. Every letter evoked memories of my time at the orphanage in Delhi and (especially) in Fakirana, and it was a beautiful experience to reread them, this time with an understanding of their context and with so much more meaning. I could picture the nuns buzzing around the Fakirana complex and then sitting down to find a few precious minutes to write and despatch letters across the seas.

Then I saw something that took my breath away. Rereading the letters written in sometimes nearly illegible handwriting, one by one, I found one that said I had been brought to Fakirana by my grandmother and uncle but also my *biological mother*, who they said was 'an unmarried Hindu girl'. She hadn't died giving birth to me after all!

I still suspect that some form of sexual assault lay behind her decision to give me up, but I have to accept that I will never know for sure. All I know is that the differences between her life and mine are so unfair. Mum was always quick to point out to me when I was growing up that my biological family's decision to take me to the orphanage so early on meant that, unlike many children in India, especially unwanted girls, there was never a day when I was deprived of love or adequate nutrition.

If I ever meet my biological mother, assuming she is still alive all these years later, there is a hell of a lot I have to thank her for. Just having me and choosing to place me in a safe and loving environment are two head starts that millions of Indian girls never get. Before my trip to India I'd expected that I would return from it doubly grateful for my Australian life, but I'd never anticipated that I'd be saying private thanks that I'd been born at all.

9

BELIEVING AND BELONGING

Along with my fate as a woman, India also confronted my deepest feelings about religion. Every Sunday when I was growing up, we Bourkes would traipse off to Mass. Early on I didn't mind this. In fact, I embraced it, even becoming an altar girl. But as I grew older, the weekly ritual became as meaningless as it was boring. Mass wasn't about God, nor was it about spirituality, it seemed to me. It was recitations, old people, and (being Bathurst) an endurance test of searing heat or freezing cold. I didn't doubt God's existence and I had a private relationship with Him that featured both peaks and valleys. But all the things we did as a Catholic family—saying grace before meals, Mass every Sunday and all the rest of it—were tiresome and repetitive.

Did I really think God was listening to every prayer before dinner or every 'Our Father' on Sunday? No. I went to Mass because we were required to. I lined up for a communion I didn't really believe was Jesus' body, sometimes closing my eyes and desperately willing myself to feel a sense of holiness. But the communion bread just left a stale, mouldy taste in my mouth and I felt no different.

By the time I was fifteen I was keeping myself amused at Mass by checking out what other people were wearing. I'd watch the worshippers walk back from the altar, mentally rating their shoes out of ten. Sometimes my older siblings would encourage the youngest ones to misbehave. If they screamed loudly enough, or couldn't be stopped running up and down the aisle, a frazzled Mum or Dad might give up altogether and bundle us back into the van for home. By sixteen I was ready to give up on church altogether, but it was one of Mum and Dad's 'under my roof' rules.

After leaving school, and now free from parental scrutiny in England, I tried to give Mass another go. I went once or twice before making it to the Christmas service, which took place not long after I arrived. But after that I let it lapse, feeling both guilty and relieved as I did so. I worried that by turning my back on the church I was sending a signal to my parents that I didn't value my upbringing. In fact, the opposite is true. I'm grateful that they're religious people and that Catholic values shaped our family life. They're the least materialistic people I know (something I can't pretend has rubbed off on me). They taught us the importance of tolerance and fairness and sharing, and they sent us out into the world with the objective of being the most honest and decent people we could be.

But I was willing to explore other forms of faith. When I was in my early twenties and living in Sydney, a then friend of mine became enamoured with the Hillsong evangelical church and asked me to go along with her. I agreed, partly out of friendship, partly out of some journalistic interest in the hype around and the 'cult' status of this brash new church, and partly out of a concern that by not attending church I was neglecting my spiritual self, my relationship with God and my ethical development.

I saw immediately that Hillsong had just as many faults as the Catholic Church. But because I made some friendships there I spent the best part of a year focusing on the positives. Mostly the church was filled with very well-meaning people; people I supposed were, like me, trying and perennially failing to be their best selves. It was also energising to be around young people in church for a change. At our Catholic church in Bathurst, outside of my family you could often count on one hand the number of people aged under twenty-five.

There were other differences, too. It was striking how ridiculously good-looking everyone at Hillsong seemed to be, particularly higher up in the church hierarchy. They drove slick new cars (mine was a rusting 1985 Toyota with perilously dodgy brakes), they wore lovely clothes, and everyone seemed to be a size 10—it was like *The Stepford Wives* meets *Glee*. This was the bells-and-whistles strain of religion where the service was one big performance: by the pastor, by the band and by the worshippers, who would sway, hands high in the air (I kept mine by my sides). The altar had been replaced by a stage. American pastors would be flown in to preach about how financial success was one of God's blessings, pointing to their own riches as an example. This was utterly opposed to the religious values on which I'd been raised.

My approach to religion is the same as the one I bring now to politics: whenever someone is trying to persuade you to follow them, always apply your most critical thinking. Because of this I knew I wasn't destined to stay at Hillsong. The unhealthy, obsessive focus on money was very off-putting. Financial donations are part of many religions, but I found the hard sell distasteful. I kept my hand in my pocket and didn't bring anyone else into the church, despite the pressure to recruit. At one point I was even discouraged from spending time cultivating friendships with anyone who wasn't a fellow Hillsong churchgoer.

Not long before I left for good, a friend from the church told me that some Muslims had just converted and joined and said wasn't it wonderful that they'd seen the 'right' path. 'What do you mean by right?' I asked with some trepidation.

'You know, this is the right religion,' she said.

'But you know there's no right or wrong, just different paths to the same destination, right?' I said. She could not be persuaded. I stopped going to the church soon afterwards, and many of what I had thought were good friendships quickly petered out, which was saddening but not surprising.

I half-heartedly tried a few other types of churches on and off for a year or so before giving up altogether, no longer even going to Mass at Christmas or on Good Friday. I would now describe myself as a 'Goddist' rather than someone who is religious. I like to think that we are given free will and there's some final transaction at the end to weigh up how we exercised it on earth, otherwise what's the point of it all? Why live and love, why feel pain, why be capable of great and evil things if it all just ends in the ground?

I love studying religions, but I'm less and less convinced that any of them are the window to the truth. Of course, it's so easy to be smug or critical about archaic institutions like the Catholic Church from the relative wealth and comfort of my life in Australia, to focus only on their abuses of power, mock their outdated belief systems and dismiss them as irrelevant to day-to-day life. The truth is, who needs religion when life is good, bills can be paid, holidays can be afforded and your job is enjoyable?

In Australia, religion can be sterile, compartmentalised, dull and devoid of relevance, but in India religion is every-where, and I mean *everywhere*. It informs the headscarves and modest clothing worn by the majority of the population; it's there in the photos and figurines of gods on car dashboards and the garlands or prayer beads or flowers hanging from rear-view mirrors. It determines menu choices. Temples are ubiquitous. You can set your watch by the Muslim call to prayer. In Bihar, the state where the Buddha is said to have achieved enlightenment, you can visit a tree grown from a cutting of the very tree under which he sat as he reached nirvana.

Religion is a living, thriving presence in Indian daily life. Hindus will often categorise Hinduism as a culture first and a religion second. Slums, like the famous Dharavi in Mumbai, are ordered along religious and cultural lines. In Australia it can be awkward to talk about religion, and you certainly don't ask a new acquaintance what faith they belong to. But in India it's as commonplace as asking which state you're from. No one minds.

At one point in the walking tour of Delhi we took with Satyender the former street kid, he led us along a narrow laneway. The wall on one side featured a series of pictures, painted in an almost cartoonish style, in a neat horizontal line. We were all puzzled by them until Satyender explained that they were icons of the gods—a varied selection of deities. They'd been strategically positioned here and elsewhere so people wouldn't piss against the walls of these cramped, busy thoroughfares. In India, he explained, everyone is religious, and even if a picture of a person's own god wasn't included they would respect the others and act accordingly. We marvelled at the simple ingenuity of the idea.

Someone asked Satyender what he believed, which god or gods he followed. He told us that he was an atheist but that he respected all believers and their religions and associated gods. Asked why he was an atheist, he said it was simple—there was no God to prevent his father beating him or his mother; there was no God on the streets of Delhi, where children roamed, stealing, begging, scavenging. It made perfect sense. I'd always felt so blessed, so grateful to God and the Catholic nuns who had given me the life I have, but would I still be thanking God if I lived a village life in rural India?

At Fakirana, the sisters had asked over dinner on our second night if I attended church. I shook my head and almost launched into my usual spiel about the church being outdated, institutionalised, old-fashioned, boring, dogmatic, stale, repetitive and irrelevant to modern life. But the words died on my tongue. Irrelevant? This was a claim I no longer felt I could make. The Catholic Church is most certainly the only reason I am alive and enjoying life in Australia. And I'm just one of tens of thousands this order of nuns alone has helped and continues to help. How could I tell these living examples of Christianity that there was no place for the church in my life? They didn't press me, and the conversation moved on.

India has a confounding way of impressing on you both the good and the bad aspects of religion and making you see things in a new light. What can seem primitive and pagan in Hinduism makes me see that Christianity and its rituals may be equally pointless. And while I do still strongly believe in the kind of God I was brought up with and the Christian idea of heaven, I also find myself more and more open to all possibilities, including the idea of souls recycled through some form of reincarnation.

One reason I would love to think that there is a heaven from which the souls of the departed can look down upon the living is so that Sister Hermann-Josef and the other nuns who died before I woke up to myself and visited India for the first time could know how much I cherish their memory and value what they did for me.

I've never understood the fascination many people have with tracing their lineage. My being adopted is the likely explanation for this attitude, and perhaps the arrogance of youth, but whatever the reason I just don't get the attraction, even when my nearest and dearest have tried to explain it. Dad is particularly keen on tracing his family history. He has linked up with cousins in Ireland, and uncovered distant relatives who emigrated to Australia in the nineteenth century and even attended the schools he taught at and we Bourke children would attend. To Dad this is remarkable. To me it's all 'meh' and 'so what?' Those old graves, sepia photographs and dusty birth certificates hold no interest for me. Life is defined by those around you in the present and is about looking forward, not back, isn't it?

So what is the most important thing in binding a family if not shared history and genes? For me it is love. It's the sacrifice that comes from love. It's loyalty, as our father always taught us: the courage to stand up for your family in public when required and to criticise only within. It's the perseverance and patience needed when the people you love rub you up the wrong way. Love links a family not genes. When people ask if I've ever met my 'real' parents, the first thing I tell them is that the parents who raised me *are* my real parents.

Working as a journalist, I'm all too aware that bad news sells. This isn't a recent phenomenon. It's human nature, and Leo Tolstoy touched on our lack of interest in good news in the opening lines of *Anna Karenina*: 'Happy families are all alike; every unhappy family is unhappy in its own way.' Adoptions gone wrong are the kind of bad news that has a perennial appeal, it seems.

I first encountered this when I was fifteen. I used the money from my part-time job to buy a subscription to the paper I now write for, the *Sydney Morning Herald* (as the future journalist I was sure I would become, I was very proud of the fact that I was the youngest subscriber in my school). The papers were delivered to school in the morning before roll call. Flicking through to the In Focus section one morning, I noticed an article by Adele Horin, whose work I still read with interest and admiration to this day. She had written about a group of Australians who had been adopted from Asia as babies and were all negative about the result.

While of course I respect those people's experience and viewpoint, they were very different from my own. To be fair, Horin had noted that the group was self-selecting and pointed out that it was therefore hard to know how representative their views were. Still, I was furious that someone might stumble on this article and think that it accurately described the adoption experience for everyone. I was determined to tell the other side of the story, and I posted off a letter to the editor, which was published a week later. My views now remain pretty much exactly as they were back in 1999:

In response to your article 'Adopting Identities' (Herald, September 17), I feel compelled to write my opinion to you. I am 15 years old, adopted from India, a middle child of eight, with an elder brother and sister also adopted from

India although not blood relations. I feel very strongly and positively on the issue of Asian adoption. I know that I may not be alive today if it weren't for my parents whom I think of as nothing but my parents. I feel 100 per cent Australian and have never been hurt from the few racial slurs that I have received in my lifetime. I have never felt an oddity, a misfit, or even different and I have been able to maintain a happy lifestyle, accepting that my adoptive parents are my parents and that my three brothers and four sisters are closer to me than any blood relation of mine may ever be. I simply feel that everyone should know adopting is a wonderful decision that benefits so many. I know that I would be living in poverty, if I had survived the poverty of India at all.

Mum and Dad were chuffed. Mum hates the idea that people will think she and Dad are 'good' for having adopted us, just as much as she resented it when people asked us three where we were from. My parents were both proud, not only that my letter was published, but also that I'd formed and expressed these views completely on my own.

No one's experience of adoption is the same; even Rani's or Damian's is different to mine. Everyone has their own story to tell. I can speak only for myself, but my view is that if this book informs or changes in a positive way even one person's view about inter-country adoption, it will have been worth it.

I can't shake the memory of a man I met on one of my later trips to India. It was at a Central Cottage Industries Emporium in Mumbai when I was shopping for artefacts to be shipped home. I started talking with the sales assistant and realised we were the same age. He was politely curious about why I looked Indian but couldn't speak Marathi or Hindi. When I told him I had been adopted and lived in Australia, his smile vanished. He looked up at me with the saddest eyes and said, 'I wish I'd been adopted to Australia as a baby.'

I looked away, feeling slightly sick. If I can rejoice in the outcome of my sliding door of fate, it is only logical that people like him would do the reverse. 'But you have a job here and everything, don't you?' I limply offered.

'Yeah, but it's not . . .' He trailed off; there was too much to say and none of it would make any difference. Just like anything else you love dearly, India can break your heart, over and over.

India's tourism slogan abroad is 'Incredible India', and it is a perfect catchphrase. India is incredible—incredibly confounding. It's not so much a country as a giant collision of extremes. Indecent extravagances of wealth versus harrowing scenes of poverty. Brilliant technological developments versus feudal rural life. Acceptance of different religious beliefs versus violent, sometimes deadly conflict. Billionaires in Mumbai whose mansions overlook slums that sprawl like cities. India demands that you take it as it is, which is why people tend to either love it or hate it, with nothing much in between. I left after that first visit obsessed, perplexed. It is by far the most complex and frustrating place I've ever experienced.

After we arrived home from that first trip, I felt lost back in Australia. Canberra's scrub seemed a faded backdrop to life after the hypercolour and activity in India. I couldn't stop looking at our photos. I spent hundreds of dollars buying books online on anything to do with India: *Shantaram*, *The White Tiger*, and more intellectual ones, such as Rangnekar's *The Politics of Poverty*, books on the Mughals, Alex von Tunzelmann's *Indian Summer* (about the partition of the Indian subcontinent and the end of the British Empire), and of course the works of historian William Dalrymple. The interest I'd never allowed myself to feel in the country, once unlocked, didn't arrive in a flood; it was a tsunami.

Graham and I were desperate to 'Indianise' our home so we would never forget our experience and the impact it had had on the both of us. We shipped whatever we could: crockery, statues of Shiva (one weighing 230 kilograms) back home. We were both hooked. India had grasped us and we weren't going to let it go. I was desperate to talk about India to anyone who had been there, and especially anyone who'd lived there. Its people had once seemed impenetrable to me. Now when Indian taxi drivers asked me where I was from I couldn't wait to answer the question. What would previously have prompted a hostile shutdown turned into a flowing conversation about both countries and cultures, and sometimes we'd both be disappointed when the short drive ended.

Compiling lists of where in India we wanted to go next became a pastime for Graham and me. South next time, we decided, and just over a year later we landed in Mumbai in searing heat. I was back to my normal travel self, poring over guidebooks and TripAdvisor and writing up lists of things to do and see.

One must-see was the Dhobi Ghat, where laundrymen slap clean clothes and sheets against rock. There were hundreds of them, shirtless, slapping away in heat nearing 40 degrees Celsius. After watching their efforts, I turned to Graham and said, 'You know, unless either of us comes down with a terminal illness, we can never say we have a problem in life, can we?' He agreed.

We couldn't go to Mumbai without seeing first-hand life inside one of its famed slum cities. Katherine Boo's book is about life in Annawadi, but the slum that is best set up for visitors is Dharavi, once the biggest in Asia and still one of the world's largest. While there are official private guides who make a living taking people round Dharavi, I was very conscious of trying to support as many charitable non-government organisations as we could. I'd heavily researched the best tours and decided on a company called Reality Tours. It specialises in showing tourists the 'Real India', which was the part I most enjoyed seeing, because it might have been my India.

Dharavi sprawls over a huge area—around 239 hectares (590 acres)—and estimates of how many people live there vary between six hundred thousand and one million; no one knows for sure. The figures tell the story: so many people means space is extremely tight. The flats are tiny and you could walk the length in less than ten steps. That's their entire home. But a slum is not just a slum, it is also a network of communities and mini towns within a city; a complex of homes; a hub of industries complete with factories; and a suburb in its own right, with schools, shops and gyms.

The smell of weed being smoked floated in the air as we approached the entrance from the railway station. Ten-year-old boys blew me kisses and tried to chat me up. We were shown the smaller, cramped Muslim quarters, the cleaner, roomier Hindu areas and the older Gujarati pottery premises. My appreciation for toilets was renewed when we were told there was just one toilet per 1500 people. Young boys played cricket on the rubbish heap next to the toilet block, immune to the smell.

Mini factories were everywhere. A sweatshop where they made clothes to be sold at outrageous prices in the west. A tannery where handbags, shoes and belts took on snakeskin-like prints. Plastic was collected and melted into tiny pellets to be sold to multinational companies, and steel was melted and moulded right before our eyes. Barely anyone wore protective clothing.

We were staying in a very different environment: the Taj Mahal Palace, one of India's signature hotels, ridiculously expensive and opulent. Beggar children would follow guests right up to the gates until the security guards roused at them to bugger off. We had to step over people sleeping on the street at midday. It was incredibly frustrating seeing people who felt they had no choice but to accept this brutal hardship. I wondered why the majority didn't rise up and demand better.

Graham and I have now travelled to India three times and we are already planning our next trip. We describe ourselves as Indiaphiles. As well as Delhi, Bihar, Agra and Mumbai, we have visited Kolkata, Tamil Nadu, Kerala, Kochi and Bangalore. Each trip shows us once again just how diverse India is. We relish the varied sights and experiences, the men wearing traditional *lungis* (an adjustable sarong worn at the waist) in Kerala, the visits to temples in 44-degree heat in Tamil Nadu.

One of our recent visits was to Chennai, where Rani had come from (she had already seen it for herself on a visit with Mum). As I'd earlier done in Bihar on my own behalf, I found myself looking at the women's faces to see if any looked like her. While Damian is not at all interested in going back or even hearing about my trips, Rani and I have tossed around the idea of going back together, along with Graham, or of her coming over to stay if Graham and I end up moving there sometime during the next decade.

Our favourite city so far has been Kolkata (formerly Calcutta). It had that same old India feel that we had loved about Old Delhi. Stores were hundreds of years old and had been owned by the current owners' great great grandparents and beyond. The poverty we witnessed was immense. Refugees from Bangladesh slept in tents on the side of the road. Naked children slept out in the open, and early in the morning it was nothing to see a homeless man washing himself on the side of the street. The rubbish was extreme, white plastic would cover the ground like snow. Creaky old metal buses were crammed so full all you could detect were mismatched limbs hanging out of the windows. The heat was sweltering. It was hard to feel like I could ever genuinely complain about much in life ever again. It reminded us of Old Delhi, the way it heaved with ordered chaos. And everywhere we went we met Biharis, who were always very excited to learn about my origins. It never mattered that I didn't speak their language and was really Australian on the inside; they saw some sort of kinship. 'You're Bihari Latika!' they would say. Once I might have minded, but now I loved it.

One of the best things about visiting India is seeing the changes that are moving it closer to realising its potential.

The country is making great progress in a whole range of areas. Bihar, especially, is improving by the year, having been chosen as a test state for a program known as PURA: Providing Urban Amenities (such as roads, water, electricity and communications) in Rural Areas. But progress isn't just happening on a macro scale. Ordinary people throughout India are fighting back against entrenched corruption that feeds the black-market economy and erodes trust in everyday institutions. They are trying to pull themselves up. Satyender is just one example of the success stories you can find if you look—he is now studying in the United States on a scholarship.

I have watched *Slumdog Millionaire* again since seeing India for myself and found I had a completely different reaction to it. This time it didn't upset me at all. It looked almost quaint, bearing so little resemblance to the country I now know and love that I could only marvel at the impact it had on me on first viewing. The hypercolour version of the country I had now come to know, just a little for myself, didn't match. Apart from the rubbish heaps, the vividness of the colours, the chaos of Victoria Terminus Station in Mumbai and the ramshackle layout of the Dharavi slum, I recognised little else of India in the slick, fast-paced movie. It's beautifully told, but it's just another film. I've outgrown it. What need do I have for a fictional India when I can conjure the smells, sights and sounds for myself just by closing my eyes?

But on every trip, with every lavish hotel we checked into, I knew I was able to love India as I do because I could experience its very finest. In my India, few people would dare to judge my gender, the darkness of my skin or whatever caste they wanted to think I might be. I am always conscious that this India would never have been the one that was mine if I had grown up there, in poverty. My Australian life made my Indian experiences possible in a way my birth country would never have allowed. I feel so lucky to have two magnificent countries to call my own.

I'll admit it is sometimes hard to maintain the perspective I have found in India when I'm back home, knee-deep in my Australian life, demanding this and that. I've hung three pictures from our street walk in Dharavi on our bedroom wall so that I see them when I wake up each morning and at least I start the day with the right intention. Tourists are strictly forbidden from taking photos, understandably—it's enough that the people of Dharavi allow so many gaping outsiders into their homes. So the pictures were taken by some of the children with a camera they were given to experiment with and developed into prints for sale. Much as I am intrigued by India's women, I am fascinated by India's youth—the hope for great change, which in turn, I desperately hope they will see in their lifetime.

But contrary to my initial fears, I don't feel plagued by paralysing western guilt about my inability to 'fix' India.

Instead, I want to do my bit by contributing as best I can. I am hopeful I can use my journalistic skills for the cause. One possibility is spending time in Bihar in a professional capacity, to learn more about its women and to help bring their stories to the world. I want to be a part of India, watch its growth from the inside, not just from the outer. It's a need for me now, to know more about this mighty place, with all its geographical, social and cultural diversity.

It's no exaggeration to say that my life has been changed by India. Mum always predicted that out of the three of us, I would be the one who would go back in my own stead. As an obstinate teenager I wanted to prove her wrong. She was right, of course.

Since turning thirty, I have barely been asked the once-detested 'Where are you from?' But on the odd occasion that I am, I proudly say, 'Bihar, in India.' When people follow up with 'Have you been back?', I cannot wait to tell them about my trips, about the work of the incredible nuns who forged a safe, peaceful and loving life for me in Australia, and about the work of the sisters who followed them and still toil in the heat of Fakirana and the grime of Delhi.

I say that I plan to learn Hindi and perhaps even live in India one day. Not as an Indian and not out of some thirst for cultural or spiritual awakening, but as a proud Australian who was adopted from there and who, like millions of other people across the globe, has fallen in love with the formidable force that is India.

India, always a part of my past, has become very much a part of my future.

ACKNOWLEDGEMENTS

This book is entirely a record of gratitude to all the people who have given of themselves to make my life a reality and to give me and others lives full of opportunity. Firstly to my mum and dad, Penny and John Bourke, obviously it is thanks to you that I have this life which I love so very much. Sorry for not always being the best daughter, but you should know that there is never a day when I don't give thanks, even if you don't know about it, for the life you gave us.

To my siblings, Melissa, Catherine, Rani, Damian, Dominic, Gabriela and Joseph, you are all wonderful, exceptionally talented people in your unique ways.

To Graham, thank you for travelling with me to India and especially for being with me during the coldest of nights in Bihar. This journey was all the more special because we did it together. Thank you for your support for this project and all the extra responsibilities you took on to allow this to happen.

And above all to the sisters at Fakirana and Delhi, past, present and future. You are walking lights in this world. Thank you for your work bringing life and love into the worlds of those who would not have the bright futures they enjoy today without your selfless loving care and tireless work.

And to my biological mother, may you be at peace.

RECOMMENDED READING

Abdul Kalam, A. P. J. & Singh, Srijian Pal *Target 3 Billion: PURA: Innovative solutions towards sustainable development*, Penguin Books India, New Delhi, 2011

Adiga, Aravind *The White Tiger*, Atlantic Books, London, 2008

Boo, Katherine *Behind the Beautiful Forevers*, Scribe, Brunswick, 2012

Dalrymple, William *Nine Lives: In search of the sacred in modern India*, Bloomsbury, London, 2009

Kaplan, Robert D. *Monsoon: The Indian Ocean and the battle for supremacy in the 21st Century*, Black Inc, Collingwood, 2010

Lal, K. S. *The Mughal Harem*, Aditya Prakashan, New Delhi, 1988

Nath, R. *Private Life of the Mughals of India 1526–1803 A.D.*, Historical Research Documentation Programme, Jaipur, 1994, 2nd edition

Rangnekar, D. K. *The Politics of Poverty: A study of bonded labour*, Chetana Publications, New Delhi, 1977

Roberts, Gregory David *Shantaram*, Scribe, Brunswick, 2003

Von Tunzelmann, Alex *Indian Summer: The secret history of the end of an empire*, Simon & Schuster, London, 2007